THIRD EDITION Revised

# INTRAMURAL SPORTS
## A Text and Study Guide

### Harris F. Beeman

Director of Intramural Sports and Recreative Services
Michigan State University

### Carol A. Harding

Director of Women's Intramurals
Michigan State University

### James H. Humphrey

Professor of Physical Education and Health
University of Maryland

PRINCETON BOOK COMPANY, PUBLISHERS
Princeton, New Jersey

Advisory Editor

*James H. Humphrey*
*University of Maryland*

# Contents

Contents

**Contents**

# Preface

The decision to revise and rewrite *Intramural Sports* has been based primarily upon numerous changes that have occurred in this area of physical education since publication of the second edition in 1960.

One of these important changes has been the widespread interest of girls and women that has developed in the area of intramurals in recent years. One of the features of the third edition is the greater emphasis that is placed upon the fact that intramural sports have become as important a function in the lives of girls and women as they are for boys and men. To this end, one of the outstanding persons in the field of women's intramurals has been added as a third collaborator on the text.

As in the case of the second edition, the material in the current volume is based essentially upon recent findings in the area of intramurals. A survey of the "users" of the second edition was made in an attempt to determine how the text might be improved and made more functional. Many of these recommendations have been incorporated in the present revision.

Reports of the various national conferences on intramural programs for college men and women have been drawn upon in bringing the present material up-to-date. In addition, a large number of new references have been incorporated into the various units for further reading.

Acknowledgement is expressed to those persons who participated in the survey of the second edition and to Russell Rivet and Lawrence Sierra, associate directors of intramural sports and recreative services at Michigan State University, for their contributions to the current revision.

Harris F. Beeman
*Michigan State University*

Carol A. Harding
*Michigan State University*

James H. Humphrey
*University of Maryland*

# Introduction

This book has been prepared for use in professional physical education and intramural administrative courses. It should also be of value to both high school and college personnel who are charged with the responsibility of conducting intramural programs. The book is arranged in such a way that it can be used in the professional physical education course devoted entirely to intramurals, or in courses in which intramurals and other phases of professional physical education are taught in combination.

The material has been arranged in a series of sequential units. Each unit contains an overview and summary of the topic in question, along with a number of study questions and assignments. To a certain extent, each unit may be considered as a separate entity. On the other hand, the interrelation of the units should be readily discerned. Consequently, a certain amount of overlapping is unavoidable. For the purpose of the preparation of students in professional physical education, the overlapping that does occur seems advisable since it makes possible the integration of the various units.

The study questions are a compilation of problems with which workers in the field of intramurals have been concerned at all educational levels. These questions provide a desirable basis for class discussions. The assignments are concerned with practical problems that intramural workers are likely to encounter at one time or another.

A desirable feature of the book lies in its use as a future reference when the student of physical education or recreation becomes a professional worker in the field.

# Orientation in Intramurals

## TERMINOLOGY

There are numerous terms used in connection with any program of physical education activities conducted for the students within a given institution. Some of the more common terms used to describe these services include "intramurals," "intramural athletics," "intramural sports," and "intramural activities." All of these terms have approximately the same meaning. The term "intramural," meaning "within the walls," is the word of importance. It means that the services are offered only to those within a given institution. It should be recognized, also, that intramurals place the emphasis on playing and participating and not on winning and crowning all-star performers.

## DEVELOPMENT OF INTRAMURALS

The development of intramural activities and programs came about because of the desire of college students to participate in athletic contests. The usual custom was that of promoting games between those groups already established on the campus.

The early intramural games may be considered as the forerunners of our modern interscholastic and intercollegiate competition. Even today, this is true at most institutions. To gain varsity status, sports generally go through a club and extramural period. During the early years of the eighteenth century, some of the best players organized teams and played other schools and clubs that also had teams in a particular sport. There was little or no faculty supervision; in many instances, there was active opposition by the faculty concerning student participation in these rough and vigorous exercises.

When colleges accepted the idea of a program of varsity sports, intramural activities were more or less shunted into the background. Some years later, fraternities, because of their permanent nature, and class organizations began to assume leadership in conducting games for those students not on varsity teams. However, it was not until the early part of the twentieth century that colleges began to organize intramural departments, with one person designated as the director.

One of the reasons for the growing concern for a "sports-for-all" program was related to the many problems involved in the use of equipment and facilities by the various groups. Another reason for acceptance of this type of program was the belief of coaches that more suitable varsity material could be developed from the intramural teams. Educators also believed that all students should be given recreational opportunities and that organized competitive activities should not be limited to the skillful few.

There was an added incentive for the development of intramural programs during and closely following World Wars I and II. The increased interest in athletics among returning veterans created an impetus for recreative activities. The mass athletic programs and enforced physical training included in the armed services program had given many more men an opportunity to learn and play games in which they might not have ordinarily participated. When they returned from service, many expressed a desire to participate in organized competition on the intramural level.

During the early 1970s, there was a significant shift of interest among college students from the traditional support of intercollegiate sports to support of intramural programs serving all students. Included in this shift of interest was a very significant increase in the number of women participating in a great variety of sports, ranging from touch football to paddle ball.

Women and girls have not experienced the rapid growth in intramural sports opportunities or mass athletic programs that men and boys have. The turn away from competition in sports for women, due to their commercial exploitation and ineffective leadership or control in the 1930s, led to extreme modification of game rules, and slowed the progress as compared with men's intramural and athletic programs. A change in cultural mores, and increased professional leadership among women in physical education, started a conservative, limited stage of women's sports. This period, during which there was a total separateness based on sex, lasted until the 1960s—long enough to allow development of separate intramural programs that were not equal in the scope of activities offered, administration, funds invested, or participation. Intramural programs based on the division of sexes prevented women from keeping pace in activities comparable to those made available to men and women on the same campuses. Men's programs were growing in participation and were funded more adequately by the athletic or physical education departments of the university. Women's programs, on the other hand, were dependent on department contributions, rummage sales, balloon sales, and the diligent volunteer time and effort of women's recreation associations and women's athletic associations. Women's opportunities in intramural sport currently are expanding—primarily due to central administration of intramurals for men and women.

A "sports-for-all" philosophy now not only includes all women students but is further extended to include faculty, staff, and their families. Central recreation service has become a campus supsportive service just as health service, counseling service, residence hall service, and lecture-concert service have. University recreational facilities are becoming the community recreation centers where the entire campus community is invited to participate in sport.

The growth of city recreation programs, together with intensive work by the American Association for Health, Physical Education and Recreation, the National Recreation Association, and the College Physical Education Association, helped tremendously to implement the sports-for-all concept. The National Intramural Association, specifically, has focused attention upon the need for all students to have the opportunity to participate. The financial depression during the 1930s developed an awareness of the great need for the opportunity for people to learn activities that could be used during leisure hours as well as in later life. Labor union spokesmen have heralded the coming of the four-day work week in the foreseeable future. The uncountable man-hours of leisure will demand adequate opportunity to acquire and perform recreational skills. There is a tremendous need for proper utilization and preservation of our natural recreative areas. Realization of this need has made it even more crucial to produce leaders who can guide students and others to a constructive use of natural areas.

Community recreation and family recreation have grown tremendously in the past few years. The right to a fuller and richer life for all members of society is being promoted by various tax supported and voluntary agencies. Not the least important of these agencies are the educational institutions of America. There is a growing feeling that these institutions are obligated to provide those extra-class activities, such as intramurals, which enrich student opportunities and experiences in many ways.

## THE PLACE OF INTRAMURALS IN THE TOTAL PROGRAM

A modern, well-balanced program of physical education generally consists of three phases. These phases include regular class activities, intramurals, and varsity athletics. There is no need for conflict between any of the three phases of the broad program of physical education. There is room and need for all, and if they are properly conducted, the three areas should complement each other. Consequently, there should be a place for all of these phases because only by providing a variety of activities, will the needs and interests of the greatest number of students be served. Today's extra-class activities are becoming popular and re-defined as an integral part of the curriculum rather than separate from traditional, structured learning as it once existed.

The physical education class-activities program is generally required of all of the students in the school. One of the major functions of this phase is to provide students with desirable learning experiences that will help them to acquire skills in a large variety of activities and to encourage their regular use.

The intramural program can serve well those students who have learned sports activities in the regularly required or scheduled-elective classes in the physical education program. It is a desirable situation when pupils have the opportunity to engage in the activities of a well-rounded intramural program. This opportunity is enhanced when the intramural program serves as a laboratory for the use of skills learned in the regular physical education class periods. Perhaps one of the best ways of assuring "carry-over" interest for later years lies in the proper acquisitition of skills. Consequently, by providing the opportunity for students to learn desirable skills in physical education classes—and simultaneously offering an open, available facility for individual and group workout or practice, plus the opportunity to play with those of near-equal ability in the intramural program—the school helps to develop interests that are likely to grow in importance as the student goes through life.

Studies in child development indicate that the extent to which motor skills are learned in the early years may have a distinct bearing on the later life of the individual. This should serve to substantiate the belief of many physical educators that wholesome recreative experiences should take place through properly conducted intramural programs. In this respect, it is important to remember that intramural activities should be slanted toward wholesome participation rather than merely toward winning. In this way, the activities become more recreative in nature instead of highly intensified contests.

The varsity athletic program serves the student with superior physical abilities. In other words, personnel of varsity teams may be considered the so-called "cream of the crop" in a given institution. This phase of the program differs from intramurals in that varsity teams include the most highly skilled performers, who represent the school in games and contests with other schools.

## CURRENT STATUS OF INTRAMURALS

Because of increased enrollment in the elementary school and limited personnel trained in physical education, emphasis has been placed again on the intramural program. The need to provide physical activity for large numbers of children is apparent to the classroom teacher and to the full or part-time physical educator. The new direction away from the teacher-centered, authoritarian atmosphere gives impetus to a changing concept in intramurals—allowing game play, open recreation, and available equipment, to permit more activity for children on the playground or in the indoor multi-purpose areas. Elementary children enjoy full muscle activity and team games and find, here, the first play experience with a large group. Understanding game play and comraderie in sport is cultivated at this level. Many different game experiences and many team opportunities are primary in program development.

In recent years, there has been a wide range of expansion in intramural programs at the middle and secondary school levels. The conventional team sport emphasis is still popular in the middle school, but new interest in individual sport appears to be gaining, particularly in the high schools. The secondary schools are expanding activities offered in the intramural program to include popular seasonal activity such as: skiing, riding, biking, back-packing, tennis, bowling, archery, and golf. Because of this new emphasis on individual activity, the intramural sports and activity clubs are expected to become an increasingly popular part of the total physical education program.

Teacher aides, teaching assistants, and parent volunteers are making significant contributions to recreational programs in the schools by supervising areas of play as part of their responsibilities. Administrators and teachers have welcomed this assistance in developing more comprehensive activity programs.

College and university programs of intramurals are as diverse as the campuses served. Students are no longer mere spectators, but display strong interest in becoming regular participants in sport. Administrators responsible for intramural programs on all campuses are concerned and are moving in new directions to mold an intramural concept to meet and encourage student interest and participation in physical activity. The traditional scheduled team competition and individual tournaments remain popular, but the informal "drop in and work out" is far more popular and appealing to the campus community. Sports and activity clubs have increased in number, with membership and activity as objectives for the club memberships.

The new accent and direction toward "sports for all" presents a challenge and an increased emphasis on intramural, recreative services in all educational institutions and communities.

## Questions for discussion

1. What is meant by the term "intramural"?
2. What is meant by the phrase "sports for all"?
3. How did intramural sports begin in the United States?
4. How have women's and men's intramural programs differed?
5. How did the two World Wars influence intramurals?
6. What is the relationship of intramurals to regular physical education classes and varsity athletics?
7. What is the current status of intramurals in the elementary school? The secondary school? College and universities?
8. Analyze the changing intramural concept.
9. "Sports for all," or opportunities for all people in sport and activity, requires that efforts be shared by all areas of physical education to meet this goal. Discuss responsibilities and relationships for progress in this direction.

## Assignments

1. Analyze and discuss the main factors that caused the control of athletics to shift from the students to the faculty of educational institutions.

2. Prepare a brief summary on the current status and trends of intramurals at one of the following levels:

   a. Elementary school
   b. Middle school and junior high school
   c. Senior high school
   d. College or university

3. Discuss the changing educational pschology which permits extra-class activity to become part of curricular activity.

4. Analyze the changing role of women in intramural sports.

## References

*Books*

American Association for Health, Physical Education, and Recreation. *Intramural Sports for College Men and Women.* Washington: National Conference Report, 1955.

American Association for Health, Physical Education, and Recreation. *Desirable Athletic Competition for Children.* Washington: Report to Joint Committee on Athletic Competition for Children of Elementary and Junior High School Age, 1952.

Bruner, Jerome. *The Process of Education.* Cambridge, Massachusetts: Howard Press, 1966.

Carlson, Reynold E., et al. *Recreation in American Life.* Belmont, California: Wadsworth Publishing Company, Inc., 1963.

Humphrey, James H. *Elementary School Physical Education,* chapter 4. New York: Harper and Brothers, 1958.

Kleindeinst, Viola, and Weston, Arthur. *Intramural and Recreation Programs for Schools and Colleges.* New York: Appleton-Century-Crofts, 1964.

Leavitt, Norma M., and Price, Hartley D. *Intramural and Recreational Sports for High School and College.* New York: The Ronald Press Company, 1958.

Means, Louis E. *Intramurals: Their Organization and Administration.* Englewood Cliffs, New Jersey: Prentice Hall, Inc., 1963.

Miller, Donna M., and Russell, Kaythryn. *Sport: A Contemporary View.* Philadelphia: Lea and Febiger, 1971.

Mitchell, Elmer D. *Sports for Recreation.* New York: A.S. Barnes & Co., Inc., 1952.

Mueller, Pat, and Mitchell, Elmer D., *Intramural Sports.* New York: The Ronald Press Company, 1960.

Rice, Emmett A. *A Brief History of Physical Education.* New York: A.S. Barnes & Company, 1929.

Schurer, William W. *High School Intramural Program.* Minneapolis: Burgess Publishing Company, 1951.

Scott, Harry. *Competitive Sports in Schools and Colleges,* chapter XI. New York: Harper and Brothers, 1951.

Voltmer, Edward F. and Esslinger, Arthur A. *Organization and Administration of Physical Education.* New York: Appleton-Century-Crofts, 1958.

Williams, Jesse F.; Brownell, Clifford L.; and Vernier, Elmon L. *The Administration of Health Education and Physical Education,* 5th edition, chapter 13. Philadelphia: W. B. Saunders Company, 1958.

*Periodicals*

Anderson, Don. "Intramural Sports in a Changing Society." *Journal of Health, Physical Education, and Recreation,* November-December 1971.

Cherry, H.S. "Intramural Unlimited." *Scholastic Coach,* vol. 22, June 1953.

Ellsburg, C.D. "The Coordination of Intramurals and Inter-scholastic Athletics." *Athletic Journal,* vol. 19, September 1938.

Harding, Carol. "A Woman's View of Men's Intramural Sports." Twenty-Second Annual Conference of the National Intramural Association, 1971, pp. 39-41.

Harding, Carol. "An Informal Drop-In Activity Program" (Student Involvement in the Administration of Sports Programs). *Journal of Health, Physical Education, and Recreation,* February 1970.

Hewatt, Carolyn. "A Woman's Viewpoint of Men's Intramurals." Twenty-Second Annual Conference of the National Intramural Association, 1971, pp. 41-45.

Jones, Tom. "Needed: A New Philosophical Model for Intramurals." *Journal of Health, Physical Education, and Recreation,* November-December 1971.

Means, Louis E. "Post-War Survey of College and University Intramurals." *Athletic Journal,* vol. 28, April 1948.

Mundt, Howard G. "The Future of Intramural Programs." *Athletic Journal,* vol. 25, February 1945.

Sparks, R.E. "Athletics for All Through Intramurals." *Scholastic Coach,* vol. 23, October 1954.

Walker, Paul. "Intramural Panacea." *Scholastic Coach,* vol. 17, May 1948.

"What Constitutes an Athletics-For-All Program." *Athletic Journal,* vol. 24, June 1964.

# Philosophy and Objectives of Intramural and Recreative Services

## INTRAMURALS AND RECREATIVE SERVICES IN EDUCATION

The broad aim of education is now generally considered in terms of total growth and development of children and youth. The intramural program provides one of the many ways through which the goal of total growth and development may be attained. Therefore, when intramurals is considered as one phase of the entire educational plan, a statement of the philosophy of intramurals must take into consideration the more comprehensive area of the philosophy of education. Therefore, the guiding principles and philosophy of intramurals should parallel the principles and philosophy of general education.

In general, there are three learning products which accrue to one degree or another from participation in physical education activities. These may be considered as direct, incidental, and indirect learning products. In a sound program, these learning products should develop through participation in intramurals as well as the regular physical education activity classes.

Direct learning products are those which are the direct object of teaching. For example, passing, shooting, dribbling, and footwork are essential skills necessary for reasonable degrees of proficiency in basketball. When one learns skills to an acceptable degree, more enjoyment is gained from participation in the activity than in performing just the skills themselves. It may be stated, then, that the learning of skills is primarily one of the direct objects of teaching. However, certain incidental and indirect learning products can result from the direct teaching. The zeal of the participant to become a more proficient performer in an activity gives rise to certain of the incidental learning products. These may be inherent in the realization and acceptance of good habits of rest, relaxation, and diet, and an awareness of what constitutes healthful living and preparation of the body for top performance. Increasing focus on fitness and lifetime sport emphasizes individual responsibility in the development of the physical potential, and clearly defines the student's role of personal involvement in maintaining a level of fitness.

Attitudes may be considered in terms of behavior tendencies; when so thought of, they might well be concerned with indirect learning products. These learning products involve such qualities as sportsmanship; respect for good human and cultural relations; appropriate behavior to allow game rule and spirit to persist; attitudes toward and appreciation of certain aspects of the activity; and other factors concerned with the adjustment and modification of the individual's reactions to others. A positive sense of community results from affirmative activity with mutual respect afforded all participants or players. This particularly appropriate atmosphere allows activity to take place freely, with a sense of being welcome and enjoying the activity. If we accept that our general goal of education is the emergence of socially aware, intelligent, and fit people—capable and willing to contribute to society—the development of attitudes must be one of the most crucial objectives of intramural activities. The way in which the director conducts the program and deals with participants in resolving conflicts will determine how attitudes will be developed.

In the early 1960s, American education was reformed, and the curriculum was reconstructed to better serve students. Changing culture and the role of technology led to serious questioning of the traditional patterns of learning experiences. Curriculum revision in the schools moved from the traditional, set class of experiences toward a widely based acceptance that learning takes places in many situations in the total school and community. Areas such as journalism, drama, art, music, physical education, industrial arts—once considered as support areas to regular curriculum—are now recognized and included in the total curriculum of the school. Work experience, independent study, teacher-aide training, and vocational career training—all reflect the new direction of curriculum and attempt to permit people to have more open and meaningful learning experiences. Emphasis has been placed upon permitting the student to become independently involved with knowledge and skills and not continually dependent on external instruction or direction. The school and community are becoming laboratories for learning, and the role of intramurals and recreative services will not be static. The traditional intramural concept has changed to include many recreative services, just as the concept of general education has been projected to offer more learning opportunities to more people and at all levels of competencies. The entire area of intramurals—sports competition, club sports, and drop-in daily workouts—reflect intramural sport as a vehicle of change, with concern for developing a better system for making recreation available for all students, faculty, and staff.

## INTRAMURAL OBJECTIVES

The field of physical education is no longer looked upon as a separate entity, in terms of total growth and development of children and youth. In other words, the objectives of physical education have gradually fused with the objectives of general education to the point where physical education now is recognized as an integral part of the total education of the individual.

It is the purpose of physical education to contribute to the physical, social, mental, emotional, and recreational well-being of the school-age population. Consequently, these same objectives should be given serious consideration in the intramural program inasmuch as this activity is an outgrowth of the regular physical education class-activity program. Intramurals may be considered as one of the many pathways through which the ultimate aim of education may be pursued. Therefore, personnel responsible for intramural programs and recreative services at the secondary school and college level must have clearly in mind the objectives of general education. If this factor is taken into consideration, it is more likely that the needs of students will be more adequately met through an intramural program that is organized on the basis of valid objectives. Neglect of this factor probably would result in an indefensible program.

### Questions for discussion

1. What philosophy should we as physical educators have with regard to intramural sports?
2. To what extent should intramural sports contribute to physical, social, emotional, intellectual, and recreational objectives?
3. To what extent should the development of varsity material be an objective of intramural sports?
4. In what way is it justifiable to have spectator entertainment as an objective of intramural sports?
5. What significance does the changing view of curriculum have upon physical education and intramurals?
6. What is the relationship of physical education to intramural sports?

### Assignments

1. On the chart following page 10, list fifteen or twenty activities which you feel would be desirable in a secondary school intramural program. Rate them, on the basis of the suggested objectives

appearing at the top of the chart, with respect to the contribution they make to the development of the individual. The objectives are only suggestive, and you may use others. Use the following rating scale:

4—makes an extremely good contribution
3—makes a considerable contribution
2—makes a moderate contribution
1—makes a small contribution
0—makes no contribution.

Add the scores vertically and horizontally to determine how well your activities contribute to the objectives.

## References

*Books*

Bruner, Jerome. *The Process of Education.* Cambridge, Massachusetts: Howard University Press, 1960.

Bruner, Jerome. *The Relevance of Education.* New York: Norton and Company, Inc., 1971.

Committee on the Student in Higher Education. *The Student in Higher Education.* New Haven, Connecticut: The Hazen Foundation, January 1968.

Dietze, Gottfried. *Youth, University and Democracy.* Baltimore: The John Hopkins Press, 1970.

Greene, Thomas. *Work, Leisure and American Leisure and American Schools.* New York: Random House, 1968.

Huelte, George and Shivers, Jay. *Public Administration of Recreational Services.* Philadelphia: Lea and Febiger, 1972.

Hughes, William; French, Esther; and Lehsten, Nelson. *Administration of Physical Education.* New York: Ronald Press Company, 1962.

Kaplan, Louis. *Mental Health and Human Relations in Education.* New York: Harper & Row, 1959.

Kleindienst, Viola, and Weston, Arthur. *Intramural and Recreation Programs for Schools and Colleges.* New York: Appleton-Century-Crofts, 1964.

Mitchell, Elmer D. *Sports for Recreation.* New York: A.S. Barnes & Company, Inc., 1952.

Mueller, Pat, and Mitchell, Elmer D. *Intramural Sports.* New York: The Ronald Press Company, 1960.

Nash, Jay B.; Moench, F.J.; and Saurborn, J.B. *Physical Education: Organization and Administration.* New York: A.S. Barnes & Company, 1951, pp. 307-310.

Voltmer, Edward F., and Esslinger, Arthur A. *The Organization and Administration of Physical Education,* 3rd edition, chapter 9. New York: Appleton-Century-Crofts, Inc., 1958.

Ziegler, Earl. *Problems in History and Philosophy of Physical Education and Sport.* Englewood Cliffs, New Jersery: Prentice-Hall, Inc., 1968.


*Periodicals*

Anderson ,Don. "Intramural Sports in a Changing Society." *Journal of Health, Physical Education and Recreation,* November-December 1971.

Gerou, Nancy. "Intramural Director." *Journal of Health, Physical Education and Recreation,* May 1961.

McCoy, M.E. "Fitness Through Intramurals." *Journal of Health, Physical Education and Recreation,* vol. 28, September 1957.

Meredith, W.F. "Role of Intramural Sports in Education." *College Physical Education Association Proceedings,* 1956.

"Intramural Athletics." *National Association Secondary School Principals Bulletin,* May 1953.

Renner, Kenneth. "Essential Prerequisites for a New Intramural Program." *Twenty-Third Annual Conference of the National Intramural Association*, 1972, pp. 80-82.

Yuhasz, M.S. "Intramurals and Physical Fitness." *College Physical Education Association Proceedings*, 1959.

Name_____ Section_____

Assignment (1)

CHART FOR RATING INTRAMURAL OBJECTIVES

| Activities | strength | endurance | coordination | skill | health | emotional stability | intellectual development | sportsmanship | cooperation | leadership | followership | recreation | | | Total |
|---|---|---|---|---|---|---|---|---|---|---|---|---|---|---|---|
| | | | | | | | | | | | | | | | |
| | | | | | | | | | | | | | | | |
| | | | | | | | | | | | | | | | |
| | | | | | | | | | | | | | | | |
| | | | | | | | | | | | | | | | |
| | | | | | | | | | | | | | | | |
| | | | | | | | | | | | | | | | |
| | | | | | | | | | | | | | | | |
| | | | | | | | | | | | | | | | |
| | | | | | | | | | | | | | | | |
| | | | | | | | | | | | | | | | |
| | | | | | | | | | | | | | | | |
| | | | | | | | | | | | | | | | |
| | | | | | | | | | | | | | | | |
| | | | | | | | | | | | | | | | |
| Total | | | | | | | | | | | | | | | |

# Preliminary
# Planning for an
# Intramural Program

## THE NEED FOR PLANNING

The success of the intramural program may be considered directly proportional to the care and extensiveness of the preliminary planning which preceded it. For this reason, it is essential that an intramural program be introduced only after careful planning. Although there may be certain fundamentals basic to the formulation of all intramural programs, those conditions related to the local situation should be given foremost attention. This is a particularly important consideration for the intramural director who lacks experience in the development of intramural programs.

The person placed in charge of the program should make himself aware of all of those conditions in the community and the school that will have either a direct or indirect influence upon the operation of intramural activities. The director can do this by making a thorough analysis of the community and the school. This is almost imperative because each community has its own unique needs, problems, and policies. Corecreation activities may be regarded very differently in some communities than in others. As an illustration, splash parties and mixed sports are encouraged in some schools and banned in others.

## FACTORS TO CONSIDER IN PLANNING FOR INTRAMURALS

An analysis of the community and school involves such factors as the socioeconomic status of its citizens, present interests of adults and students, and availability of facilities. When such material as this is collected and analyzed, planning for intramurals is facilitated, and the needs and interests of those involved in the program are more likely to be met.

The intramural director should explore the present program of the community—taking into consideration its playgrounds and gymnasiums and commercial areas of skiing, ice skating, tennis, golf, and weight training. Are these facilities being used to capacity? Could the school use them? Are they near enough to the school for use? Are the programs well organized? Is there adequate supervision? What activities does the community offer? Are there people in the community who are interested in serving as resource people in various areas of activity? These and countless other questions may be answered when an analysis of the community is made.

In analyzing the school, the director should be concerned with such factors as the present use of all available playing areas, how the time is divided with varsity teams, and the time the students are available and facilities are needed. The size of the school enrollment must be known because this may determine largely the type of program that may be offered. In studying the school situation, it is also important to survey the interests of staff personnel concerning the intramural program. If the interests of some of the teachers can be stimulated, they may be able to make certain worthwhile contributions to the program. Faculty and staff members in the school may be able to make contributions to special activity interests of particular groups of students. For example, the music teacher who is an avid fencer might welcome the opportunity to become involved with a group interested in fencing. Many faculty members, administrators, or parents could be fine activity resource people. Their interest in contributing time and effort will be determined by the concern and interest of the administrator of intramurals.

## A SAMPLE COMMUNITY AND SCHOOL ANALYSIS

The sample analyses which follow may be used as a guide for the assignments in this unit. Certain deficiencies will be noted in this hypothetical situation. Consequently, class members should subject it to critical appraisal and evaluation because it is written in insufficient detail.

## COMMUNITY ANALYSIS

Blanktown is located in Southwestern State, twelve miles east of the city of Metropolis. The population is approximately 9,000. In the early twenties, Blanktown had several small manufacturing organizations. However, during recent years, it has become more of a residential district since a greater part of its inhabitants work in the city of Metropolis.

Community facilities for recreation include a church gymnasium, which is used for the most part by the local Y.M.C.A. This group promotes such activities as table tennis, a softball league during the summer months, and various hobby activities for adults. There are two privately owned bowling alleys that have league championships for men and women. The teams are sponsored by local merchants, and the league is conducted on a handicap basis in order to equalize competition. The community also supports teams in basketball, league baseball, and bowling, which compete with other teams made up from other Metropolis suburbs.

The high school physical education department sponsors an alumni basketball league in the winter months. There are usually six teams in this league, and it is conducted on a double round-robin basis.

## SCHOOL ANALYSIS

Blanktown high school is a six-year system, with an enrollment of between 950 and 1,000 boys and girls. There is an equal distribution between boys and girls. There is a director of physical education for girls and a director of physical education for boys.

Facilities include an athletic field, which is about three quarters of a mile away from the school, two gymnasiums, and a small playground, next to the school, which has been made into a softball diamond. There is an indoor running track, of twenty laps to the mile, encircling the boys' gymnasium. The athletic field includes one football field, a quarter-mile running track, one baseball diamond, two tennis courts, and two horseshoe-pitching courts. Supplies such as balls, nets, and other material are quite sufficient for the physical education program.

About one-half of the students come to school on school buses, and leave right after school is over in the afternoon. The rest of the pupils are within walking distance of the school.

**Questions for discussion**

1. What community factors should be considered in the development of an intramural program?
2. What school factors should be considered in the development of an intramural program?
3. What factors should be considered in utilizing commercial or municipal facilities for the intramural program?

## Assignments

1. Make an analysis of a community with which you are familiar, taking into consideration the possibility of developing an intramural program in that community. Write this analysis in the space provided in the back of the book.

2. Do the same for a school within the community, taking into consideration present use of facilities, time students are available, and other factors which would influence the development of an intramural program. Write this analysis in the space provided in the back of this book.

## References

*Books*

Huelte, George and Shiers, Jay. *Public Administration of Recreational Services.* Philadelphia: Lea & Febiger, 1972

Means, Louis E. *Intramurals—Their Organization and Administration.* New York: Prentice-Hall, Inc., 1963.

*Periodicals*

"Intramurals for College Men and Women." American Association for Health, Physical Education, and Recreation, Washington, D.C., 1964.

"Intramurals for the Senior High School." Athletic Institute, Chicago, 1964.

Elbel, E. R. "Intramural Athletics for High School Boys." *Athletic Journal,* vol. 22, April 1942.

Howell, F. E. "Intramural Physical Education Program." *Athletic Journal,* vol. 36, January 1956.

Nord, G. E. "Intramural Program in Junior High School Activities." *School Activities,* October 1955.

Simpson, Malin. "Intramurals for Boys in a Large Junior High School." *Journal of Health and Physical Education,* vol. 19, December 1948.

Watkins, James H. "Intramurals in the Junior High School." *Journal of the AAHPER,* vol. 21, May 1950.

# Organization and Administration of the Intramural Department

## SCOPE OF ORGANIZATION AND ADMINISTRATION

Organization is generally concerned with arranging a group of parts which may be dependent on one another into one whole. In this case, organization provides the machinery that makes an intramural program function. Administration is related to the process of adequately conducting the program after it has been organized. Administering involves people, places, materials, and time. It is the melding of diverse skills, activities, areas, and people to accomplish joint goals.

The administrator provides two diverse and yet overlapping and similar functions—direction and service. This individual provides direction by offering ideas, suggestions, and a basic philosophy—such as the philosophy of student service. He or she also directs by relinquishing and delegating authority as well as responsibility to the staff.

The administrator provides service by clearing obstacles on his level to enable the staff to accomplish their responsibilities. Service is also provided by insuring open communication and an efficient clearing house for requests and proposals among all staff members and by making decisions within reasonable time periods.

The greatest responsibility of the administrator is to establish and maintain an effective human relations atmosphere among the staff. Efficiency in an intramural program is not as important as the relationships that are generated between the staff members and between the staff and participants.

A philosophy that encourages the staff to attack the problems that individuals have—not the individuals that have the problems—helps to insure that people receive greater consideration than matters such as schedules and materials.

When individuals become administrators they must realize that attaining that position does not mean attaining privileges—it means service and responsibility to the staff and the participants involved in the program.

Because of the many factors that influence intramurals at various grade levels, no one organizational plan can be recommended for all situations. In organizing the program, such considerations as personnel, facilities, and school enrollment will determine to a large extent the type of organization that is best adapted to the circumstances. There are, therefore, many plans and combinations of plans for the organization and administration of intramurals. In this regard, it should be understood that the types of organizational plans and administrative procedures recommended here are merely examples of some of the more common types found in operation in current intramural programs.

## TYPES OF ORGANIZATION AND ADMINISTRATION

Whenever possible, it seems advisable to have all phases of the physical education program under the directorship of one individual who coordinates the various activities of the total program. In this type of organization, it is a general practice for the director to delegate the responsibility for conducting the intramural program to a staff member best fitted for this job in terms of interest, training, and experience. This plan may be found in operation most often at the college level, although it is used successfully in some large high schools. The extent of other responsibilities that the person in charge of intramurals may have depends largely upon the size of the school. In most cases at the junior or senior high school level, the intramural director has numerous other duties to perform.

In the public schools, any one of a number of persons may be asked to accept the responsibility for the direction of intramurals. It is a common practice to delegate this responsibility to the director of physical education, a varsity coach, or a teacher in another area of study. Again, depending upon the size of the school and the administrative philosophy, it is possible that one person may perform any combination of the functions of a physical education director, coach, or academic teacher. The physical education director may also coach; a coach may be a physical education teacher or an academic teacher, or both. However, in other instances, the physical education director has little or no varsity coaching responsibility. It should be borne in mind that, whenever possible, the best qualified person should be selected to take charge of the intramural program. This person should be chosen on the basis of interest, training, and experience, for it is clearly evident that often the success of intramurals is dependent upon the person in charge of the program. It has been shown in numerous situations that intramural participation fluctuates upward or downward in an almost direct proportion to the zeal and interest that the director has for the program. With these factors in mind, the following discussion is concerned with advantages and limitations of having each of the previously mentioned personnel responsible for the intramural program.

### The Physical Education Director

High school physical education and athletic staffs often consist of teachers who combine the coaching of varsity sports and the teaching of physical education classes. In some cases, however, one person may be employed for the sole purpose of directing the physical education program and assuming all, or a part of, the responsibility for the teaching of physical education. This is a sound plan in that it is more likely to reduce the conflict that might exist between the time for class work and the time for coaching. When this situation is employed, it is a common practice to have a man in charge of the boys' program and a woman in charge of the girls' program.

There are a number of features which point up the desirability of having the physical education director responsible for the intramural program. The man and woman directors should be familiar with all of the facilities and equipment used by both boys and girls. Scheduling of the various activity areas is a necessary part of their job. Corecreational activities can be more easily arranged because of an established working relationship between the directors of the boys' and girls' departments. The physical education director knows the long-range goals of the program, and he or she should be able to plan intramural activities that complement the regular physical education classes. In other words, the planning of intramural activities could be coordinated with the skills taught in the physical education classes. Moreover, in this kind of organization, an efficient plan of conducting some of the intramural activities during the regular physical education class hour could be devised without detracting from either of these phases of the entire program of physical education.

When the physical education director has the main responsibility for providing the intramural activities for a school, he or she should be able to plan a much more comprehensive program in every way. Each year the program could improve, and the organization and administration remain stable, with the award and point systems staying continous and uniform. Competition can progress smoothly from one season to the next, with the use of the various types of tournaments best suited to each activity.

It should be remembered that many of the advantages of this type of organization might not be realized if the physical education director is given full responsibility for the intramural program without proper adjustment of teaching load and other duties. If the intramural duties are added to an otherwise full schedule, it is possible that all phases of the program might not function to their greatest potential. For example, the physical education classes might become merely intramural contests and teams might be formed only from these classes.

## The Varsity Coach

In some high schools, it is a common practice to have one of the varsity coaches assume the responsibility for the intramural program. Sometimes the coach is allowed time for this work by a reduction in the teaching load. The intramural duties may be arranged so that they do not conflict with his or her coaching responsibilities.

With such an arrangement, it is possible that during the coaching season there will be fewer activities for intramural participants. It is not always convenient or possible for the coach to divide his time and best efforts equitably between two such demanding jobs as coaching a varsity team and conducting an intramural program. As a consequence, one is likely to be slighted at the expense of the other. Because of public interest and widespread publicity for varsity sports for boys and girls, the intramural program is frequently neglected. Furthermore, the individual whose greatest interest lies in the area of coaching varsity teams may be inclined to look upon the intramural participants solely as possible varsity candidates. When this occurs, the coaches are likely to direct most attention to the better intramural performers rather than concerning themselves with the greater mass of students with lesser abilities.

In some instances, the task of operating the intramural program is divided among several coaches. The value of this plan, as far as coaches are concerned, is that the coaches work in the intramural program during the season that their teams are not in action. However, if coaches take turns during their off-seasons, it is necessary to establish satisfactory coordination and cooperation between them. Otherwise, for example, one might favor single-elimination contests, while another might think round-robin play is best. If awards are to be purchased, they must be ordered ahead of time; therefore, the coach in charge during one season would have to order awards for the coach who was to follow him. The finances would have to be carefully budgeted so that the coaches operating the intramural program during the fall and winter seasons would leave a sufficient amount of financial support for the coach who has charge of the spring intramural activities.

If all other factors were equal, there might still remain the problem of individual differences among personnel with respect to multiple responsibility for the program. The intramural participants might not have sufficient time to get fully accustomed to one director before another person assumed charge. This would, perhaps, make for difficult coordination with the student leaders involved in the program.

One of the desirable features of having a varsity coach in charge of the intramural program is that usually he or she is well known and personally admired by the student body. If their time and interests were not divided, most coaches would no doubt make outstanding intramural directors. The bulk of their time, however, is demanded by the pressure of providing winning varsity teams.

Although there are situations where this plan of operation is successful, in other cases it leaves much to be desired. This does not imply that the varsity coach does not have a significant place in the intramural program. On the contrary, the ultimate success of the intramural program should be a responsibility of all members of the physical education and athletic staff. Perhaps one of the most useful roles of the varsity coach is in the additional instruction they may render in the skills, techniques, and strategy in their particular sport. If clinics or special instruction periods could be arranged before certain phases of intramural competition begins, the coaches, as well as the intramural participants, would profit greatly.

## The Other Teachers

In some places, successful intramural programs have been carried on with another teacher in charge of the program. One of the disadvantages of this plan is that oftentimes other teachers do not have the background of training commensurate with duties of the intramural director. However, this can be compensated for, to a certain extent, when the teacher has a high degree of interest for the position and is willing to do some independent study and to learn on the job, and also by encouraging the contribution of staff with more competence in particular areas.

## STUDENT MANGERS

Most intramural departments employ some sort of student-management system. More often than not, the success of the program is highly dependent upon a well-organized corps of student managers who give invaluable assistance to the intramural director. The values inherent in this practice are two-fold. First, the students have the opportunity to learn how to assume responsibility and to recognize the importance of worthwhile service. Second, the service of student managers is almost indispensable to the functioning of a successful intramural program. And it should not be forgotten that, since the intramural program is set up for the students, the students should be encouraged to assume an active part in its management, operation, and planning.

There are a number of satisfactory methods of obtaining student managers for service in the program. Some of these include voluntary action on the part of students, selection of students by the intramural director, and popular vote of the student body. In some cases, a combination of these methods is used.

In general, student leadership is in evidence in two ways: first, as a worker and helper for the intramural department; and second, as a unit manager responsible for a group or team. The following list includes some of the duties that a manager working with the intramural department may be called upon to perform:

1. Help with scheduling
2. Conduct individual athletic contests
3. Distribute notices and other information
4. Collect team rosters
5. Supervise play areas
6. Issue and collect equipment
7. Keep records
8. Check eligibility of participants
9. Officiate at games

The unit or team managers may be expected to perform many of the following functions:

1. Organize group into teams
2. Enter team roster for competition
3. Check eligibility of participants
4. Attend intramural rules' meetings
5. Notify teams of schedules, postponements, and forfeits
6. Check out equipment
7. Obtain practice time and space
8. Furnish scorers, timers, judges, and other officials when necessary
9. Promote all intramural activities among the group

## INTRAMURAL COUNCIL OR COMMITTEE

It has been found, through experience, that intramural programs function to a high degree of proficiency when an intramural council or committee assists in the organization and administration of the program. When this group serves in an advisory capacity, principles of democratic organization are in evidence.

Representation on the intramural council or committee may include the school administration, the physical education department, faculty members, student managers, unit managers, and others who can make a satisfactory contribution. This group can be divided into various subcommittees, such as an equipment committee, a protest committee, and others that seem necessary to the proper administration of the program.

## ORGANIZATION AT THE COLLEGE AND UNIVERSITY LEVEL

In colleges and universities, the practice of placing the control of the program under one individual is far more advanced and more frequent than in secondary schools. Oftentimes, they are in a better position financially, with better facilities and more comprehensive programs to be administered, and an intramural director is appointed. In many cases, the directors are also physical education instructors and varsity coaches or varsity coaches only. Current direction is toward single administrative responsibility for intramurals. As programs and participation have increased and campus enrollment multiplied, there is an evident concern for appropriate intramural departments responsible for continual adequate planning to meet the campus needs for recreational activity. The multi-university, or the college or university with an enrollment of 8,000 students or more, has the pressing need to encourage respect for student identity, and place more emphasis on effective community recreation service to serve the individual student's interests in a positive, responsive program of sport and activity. Large residence hall complexes, multiplying off-campus dwellings and cooperatives—all encourage more team and individual involvement with university recreation services. This service demonstrates the university's interest—and their investment in establishing a rapport with the students and total interest in their membership in the university community.

Intramurals and recreation provide integral community services, and the college or university benefits from such affirmative participation. Complete coordination of facilities with physical education and athletics remains the responsibility of the director of intramurals. Utilization of all facilities and equipment to best serve all students is in the best interest of the college or university.

Usually the intramural program at the college level is a part of the department of physical education and athletics. However, there is a trend at the college level to have the intramural programs report directly to the vice-president or chancellor of student affairs.

## SOME SAMPLE PLANS OF INTRAMURAL ORGANIZATION

Some sample plans of intramural organization are presented in Figures 1, 2, and 3. It should be borne in mind that each school situation presents certain unique problems which will govern the best type of organizational plan for the specific school. For this reason, it is recommended that the student use the plans presented here as a guide in formulating his own intramural organization chart.

### Questions for discussion

1. What are some advantages of intramurals organized under a unified administrative unit? How does this plan function in secondary schools? In colleges and universities?
2. How do intramural managers fit into the organizational plan in secondary schools?
3. At the secondary school level, what is the place of the following persons in the intramural organizational plan: principal, varsity coaches, director of physical education, student leaders?
4. How should an intramural council or committee function in the administration of an intramural program at the secondary school level? At the college and university level?
5. Discuss the administrator's role in effectively working with people.

### Assignments

1. Devise an intramural organization chart for the school of which you made an analysis in the assignment in Unit III. Any of the sample charts in the references may be used as a guide.

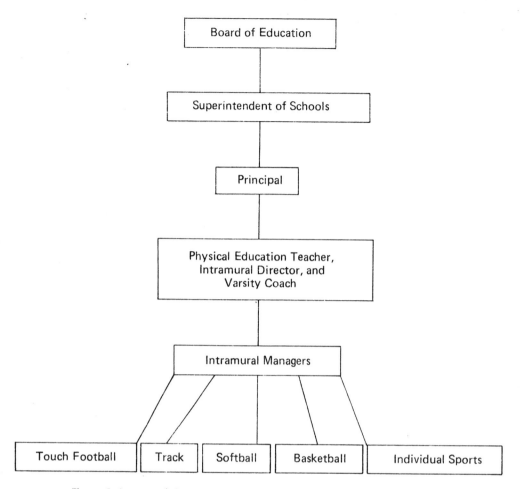

**Figure 1.** Intramural Organizational Plan for a Small Four-Year High School

2. Make a list of eight or ten administrative duties that you believe should be performed by the person in charge of a secondary school program.

## References

*Books*

Hughes, William L., and Williams, Jesse F. *Sports: Their Organization and Administration.* New York: A. S. Barnes & Company, 1944, pp. 134-139; 285-290.

Irwin, Leslie W. *The Curriculum in Health and Physical Education.* 2nd edition, chapters XI, XII, XIII. St. Louis: The C. V. Mosby Company, 1951.

Leavitt, Norma and Price, Hartley D. *Intramural and Recreational Sports for High School and College.* 2nd edition, chapter III. New York: The Ronald Press Company.

Gerber, Ellen. *Innovators and Institutions in Physical Education.* Philadelphia: Lea and Febiger, 1971.

*Periodicals*

Caldwell, Stratton, and Dalis, Peter. "The American Intramural Sports Program in Institutions of Higher Learning." *The Physical Educator,* December 1964.

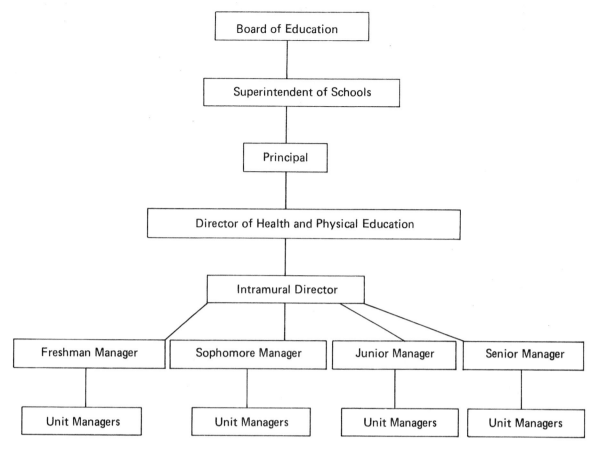

**Figure 2.** Intramural Organizational Plan for a Large Four-Year High School

Harding, Carol, and Sliger, Ira. "Student Involvement in Administration of Sports Programs." "An Informal Drop-in Program. "Extensive Sports Club Program." "Student Aquatic Center Recreation Complex." *Journal of Health, Physical Education and Recreation,* February 1970.

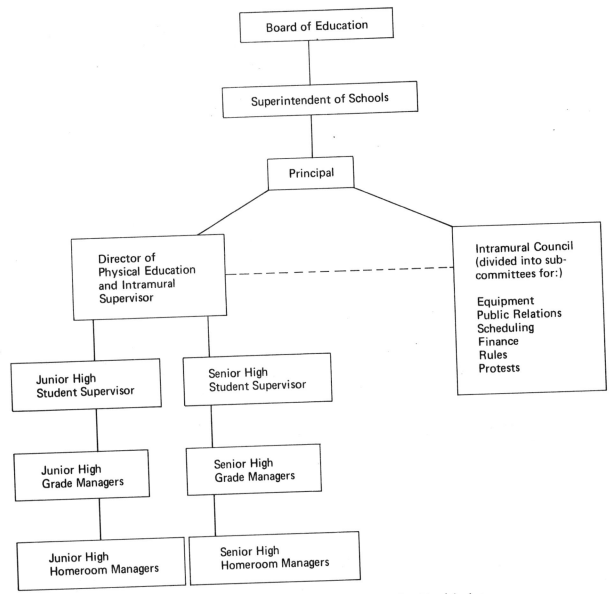

**Figure 3.** Intramural Organizational Plan for a Six-Year Combined Junior-Senior High School Showing the Function of the Intramural Council

# Scope of
# Administrative Responsibilities and
# Special Problems

There are numerous problems connected with the successful administration of an intramural program. Each school is unique to the extent that certain problems manifest themselves in a way peculiar to the specific situation. For this reason, there can be no standardized method of solving all administrative problems. However, there are a number of administrative responsibilities which are common to many schools. Some recommendations for handling many of these problems are presented in the discussions which follow.

## SAFEGUARDING THE HEALTH OF PARTICIPANTS

In the early development of the intramural movement there was considerable emphasis placed on the number of students that could be listed as having participated in the intramural program. In an effort to increase the number of participants, the welfare of the students was sometimes neglected. In some cases, more thought was given to the number of students entered in the various activities than was given to the health and physical condition of the students who participated.

As intramural programs progressed and the values that were involved became better known and appreciated, individuals responsible for the programs became increasingly concerned about the welfare of the individual student. They found that if the activities were conducted in a worthwhile maner, and if safeguards were adopted to protect the health of students, a great many students would enthusiastically participate.

Whenever possible, it is highly desirable for intramural participants to have a complete physical examination. Colleges generally have some method of examining all entering freshmen. Although this procedure may not be an infallible safeguard for the student during his four years of college, it does serve the purpose of detecting those students whose programs should be modified.

At the high-school level, it is a common practice to provide physical examinations for boys and girls who plan to compete in interscholastic athletics. This same practice is not widespread for intramural participants, but it is a procedure which is highly recommended as a health and safety measure.

Although a complete physical examination is a basic requisite in the health protection of intramural participants, other measures should also be taken to help to insure the safety and well-being of students. These measures concern such factors as proper supervision of activities, periodic examination of playing areas and equipment for safety hazards, and preseason practice for vigorous types of activities.

A capable supervisor should always be present during an intramural contest. At the college level, an experienced junior or senior student may well perform this duty. In high schools, this responsibility should be assigned to a faculty member. It is very important that a well-defined procedure be planned to take care of every injury, regardless of its extent. A complete first-aid kit, easily accessible, should be available and ready for use if needed. The supervisor should understand clearly the school policy with respect to injuries and first aid so that the proper procedures may be followed. If there is a school-accident report form to be filled out, it is the duty of the person in charge to take care of this matter. If there is no school accident report form, there should be some type of accident reporting device for use in the intramural department.

Another precaution which may be taken as a safeguard against serious injury concerns preseason practice for vigorous activities such as wrestling and cross country. In schools where this practice is in effect, the requirements vary from at least five supervised workouts to weeks of practice before the events.

Even though serious injuries are rare in intramural activities, there should be some method of protection for students who sustain accidents of a serious nature. Numerous insurance plans are now available for participants. In some cases, commercial insurance companies have expanded coverage for interscholastic athletes which includes intramural participants. This situation also prevails in some states where athletic insurance coverage is provided by the State Athletic Association for member schools. In other instances, the local school may have its own plan for protecting participating students.

## LIABILITY FOR ACCIDENTS

With the increase in intramural and recreation programs providing greater opportunity for informal unorganized activities, there has been an increase in the chance for personnel to be held legally responsible for injuries of participants. Each individual should determine the law concerning injury through negligence in his state and school system.

In general, teachers, coaches, and supervisors are not liable if they can prove they were not negligent. Negligence is commonly determined as the failure to act as a reasonably prudent and careful person would act. In some instances, it may be determined that failure to act at all was negligence.

It is important to note that those individuals with special skills are expected to act at a higher level of prudence than a layman with no special knowledge. Thus, a lifeguard could be held for greater responsibility than another person without a lifesaving certificate. A coach or physical education teacher would be expected to have more knowledge than others about the danger of certain vigorous activities and the use of certain equipment or apparatus.

An intramural director who allows students to use a trampoline or weight-lifting equipment without supervision might be vulnerable if a participant were injured while using the equipment. Signs or posters warning of the danger, or forbidding use of areas or equipment, do not necessarily relieve the director of this responsibility. However, the participant is expected to carry some responsibility for his or her actions. If contributory negligence is proved—that is, with both parties at fault—the responsibility of the teacher or director is at least legally reduced. The student, too, is held responsible for reasonably prudent action for a person of his age and experience. Regardless of legal responsibility, the greater moral responsibility for the protection of participants should motivate the intramural director to provide safe areas, equipment, and activities.

There are some activities in which there is inherent injury because of their nature. If the rules governing the activity are reasonable; if the areas and equipment are safe; if adequate supervision or officiating is provided; and if the student participates by his own consent, negligence could be difficult to prove. If, however, the director required the student to use faulty equipment or dangerous fields or courts, then negligence could be shown.

In activities such as touch football, hockey, basketball, and other vigorous or body contact sports, written instructions, rules, and meetings with supervisors, managers, and officials should emphasize the reason for certain safety rules and regulations. Constant inspection of fields and courts to identify dangerous conditions will help protect both the participant and the director.

## SERVICES FOR "HANDICAPPERS"

The term, "handicapper," for purposes of this discussion, pertains to those individuals who have certain physical limitations. This designation for those who have a physical handicap is suggested by the National Association of Physically Handicapped. Sound intramural philosophy indicates that provision should be made for all students to participate in activities fitted to their needs and interests.

It is of critical importance that those responsible for planning recreative facilities and services involve a handicapper in the initial stages of the planning. Contact should be made with the local chapter or the headquarters of the National Association of Physically Handicapped for suggested building specifications. This foresight will prevent obstacles and inconveniences such as curbs, steps, and rest room fixtures and mirrors at unreachable heights from denying these participants easy access to the recreative facilities. Safety is also involved. For example, every outside entrance should be accessible, not just one. In the event of fire, handicappers should have the same opportunity to escape as all participants.

There is usually a small percentage of students who have some type of physical impairment which prohibits them from taking part in regular types of activities. There are numerous kinds of activities that can be arranged for persons with physical limitations, and if necessary, a restricted program with modified activities can be devised for these students. A suggested program of this nature is discussed in greater detail in Unit X. In all instances, a medical doctor should make the decision as to the amount and type of activity that is appropriate for the handicapped participants.

Students should not be placed in restricted intramural programs automatically. In other words, it is strongly recommended that, whenever possible, the exceptional students should be permitted to take part in the regular intramural program. It seems a wise policy not to segregate students if this can be avoided. The reason is obvious, because one hears daily of individuals who have made very satisfactory adjustments to society in spite of their physical limitations.

## SHOWER AND LOCKER ROOM SUPERVISON

A potentially unsafe area in any educational institution is the shower and locker room. First, there is danger of injury from slipping on wet and slippery floors, and, second, there is the danger of foot and skin infections.

Student managers can be assigned to help the custodian maintain reasonable cleanliness in the locker area. Such things as running and playing in the shower room should not be allowed. Supervision may be made available through student managers or the faculty intramural staff. Education of the participants with respect to the values of cleanliness should do much to increase locker room sanitation and safety in the shower room. This can be accomplished, in part, by having intramural participants help to formulate policies for safety and cleanliness in the locker and shower areas.

## EQUIPMENT AND SUPPLIES

There are various ways of providing necessary equipment and supplies for use in the intramural program. The way in which materials are made available for intramural activities will depend largely on the amount of financial support available for this phase of the program. In many small high schools, the same materials are used for varsity athletics, physical education classes, and intramurals. This is a feasible plan if there is an equitable distribution of the materials and if the condition of the materials is satisfactory. The materials used for intramurals should be in as good condition as materials used for other phases of the program. When this procedure is adhered to, there is less likelihood of the intramural program operating with "hand-me-down" supplies.

An optional feature, in terms of equipment for intramurals, is the uniform or suit requirement for participation. In some localities, it is felt that the intramural participant should be required to wear a regulation intramural uniform. There appears to be little advantage to this requirement other than uniformity in outward appearance. When this procedure is followed, however, there must be some method of supplying the uniforms. If the school is unable to furnish them, the responsibility falls on the students. If an individual cannot afford a uniform, its lack might prevent his participation.

The main consideration with regard to intramural dress should be in terms of cleanliness, appropriateness, and identification of teams and participants. If the school furnishes different-colored jerseys to identify teams, then sufficient provision should be made for laundering so that participants will be assured of clean equipment.

In most instances, at the public school level, participants use the same uniforms or activity clothing for intramurals that they use in the regular physical education classes. This plan is a desirable one if the necessary precautions with respect to cleanliness are taken into consideration. Uniformity in dress for activity is not popular, and many students are requesting that there should be no uniform requirement. This places more responsibility on the intramural participant to wear comfortable, clean, and appropriate clothing for activities. If there is a standard uniform used for regular classes, intramural teams may be identified by arm bands, sashes, "pinnies," or some similar device.

## OFFICIALS

The four main sources of intramural officials are varsity athletes, other students, classroom teachers, and physical education and coaching staff members.

A large number of successful intramural programs rely on the services of students as officials. The desirability of this plan lies in its promise of having more student participation. By and large, varsity athletes make good student officials because they have a fairly good understanding of the rules and a genuine interest in the activity. Furthermore, this practice provides good training for the athlete and makes for better coordination between intramurals and interscholastic athletics.

However, it should be borne in mind that just because an individual is a varsity member, it does not necessarily follow that he will be an outstanding official. It is not a wise policy to confine student officiating to varsity athletes. Oftentimes students who are not on the varsity do a very commendable job of officiating because of their interest in the activity, knowledge of the rules, and judgment in decisions. In this regard, numerous successful intramural programs have, as a part of the program, an officials' club for the purpose of handling the qualifications. In some cases, officials' classes and clinics are held, and regular meetings are conducted for rules' interpretations.

When a major part of the officiating can be handled by students, faculty officiating should perhaps be kept at a minimum. It seems best to use faculty members as officials only at their own volition rather than imposing this job upon them. In this connection, it is not uncommon to have faculty members who have had previous experience in certain sports activities volunteer their services as officials.

## RECORDS AND REPORTS

If an intramural program is to function adequately, there should be some satisfactory method of record keeping and reporting. This is essential for evaluation of the program in terms of eliminating unsatisfactory practices and effecting general program improvement.

There is a need for an annual report by the intramural department concerning the number of activities offered and the number of times that students participate in the activities. There should be reports regarding the number and extent of injuries sustained in intramurals. This helps to provide for better safety measures. Reports in the form of an equipment inventory, in addition to a financial statement of the intramural department, should be made periodically so that the current status of the department may be ascertained when necessary.

It is advisable for the person in charge of the program to devise his own forms for use in keeping records and making out reports. This is necessary so that the forms used will conform to the specific conditions involved in the local situation.

## Questions for discussion

1. What methods may be used for health supervision in intramurals at the secondary school level?
2. What are some ways of providing for first aid and care of injuries in intramurals?
3. How can provisions be made for exceptional students in the intramural program?
4. What provisions should be made for locker room and shower supervision?
5. What provisions should be made for preseason practice for certain activities?
6. What are some of the problems in the care of equipment for intramurals?
7. How can officials be obtained at the secondary school level? At the college level?
8. Should there be uniform or suit requirements for the participants?
9. What are some administrative responsibilities with regard to records, forms, and reports?

## Assignments

1. Devise an original form which you feel might be useful in some phase of the intramural program at the secondary school level. Consult the references for sample forms.

2. Plan a procedure that should be followed by an intramural worker when a player is injured during a game.

## References

*Books*

Kleindienst, Viola, and Weston, Arthur. *Intramural and Recreation Programs for Schools and Colleges.* New York: Appleton-Century-Crafts, 1964.

Leavitt, Norma, and Price, Hartley D. *Intramural and Recreational Sports for High School and College,* chapter VII. New York: The Ronald Press Company, 1958.

Means, Louis E. *Intramurals: Their Organization and Administration.* Englewood Cliffs, New Jersey: Prentice-Hall, 1963.

Voltmer, Carl D., and Lapp, Vernon W. *The Intramural Handbook,* chapter II. St. Louis: The C. V. Mosby Company.

Williams, Jesse F.; Brownell, Clifford L.; and Vernier, Elmon L. *The Administration of Health Education and Physical Education,* 5th edition, chapter 13. Philadelphia: W. B. Saunders Company.

*Periodicals*

Delano, A. L. "Shall We Officiate Our Own Games." *Journal of Health-Physical Education-Recreation,* vol. 27, November 1956.

Dzenowagis, Joseph, and Sierra, Lawrence. "Injuries in Intramural Sports." *Journal of Health, Physical Education and Recreation,* September 1972.

Glascott, J. A. "Intramural Officiating." *College Physical Education Association Proceeding,* 1955.

Grambeau, R. J. "Developing Safety in Intramural Sports." *College Physical Education Association Proceedings,* 1956.

Grambeau, R. J. "Medical and Surgical Care for Injuries and Insurance." *College Physical Education Association Proceedings,* 1955.

Keen, P. V. "Problems Related to the Conduct of Intramural Sports Programs." *College Physical Education Association Proceedings,* 1956.

Sierra, Lawrence. "Presenting Injuries in College Intramural Sports." *Journal of Health, Physical Education, and Recreation,* September 1972.

Tucker, R. "Intramural for Thousands." *Scholastic Coach,* October 1952.

# Human Relations and the
# Case Method in
# Administration

For the efficient administration of any type of program, the responsible individual must recognize the limitless relationships involved in every action and decision. Some of these relationships include the director with his various faculty and department colleagues and assistants; or relationships among supervisors themselves and with the director; or the director with participants, officials, and managers. All these people interact, not only with the director but in innumerable combinations with each other and the hundreds of additional individuals with whom they have contact.

The director who can more readily discern the cause of a problem—the real issues involved—can more quickly come to an intelligent, efficient solution.

How does a potential intramural director learn to administer a program? He can learn the techniques of schedule making and organizational planning and the method of devising an equitable point system from textbooks and other literature. It is much more difficult to learn how to make a wise and fair decision in an emotionally charged problem of eligibility, with flagrantly abusive players, or in conflicting reservations involving other school departments.

Perhaps the next best experience to encounter in lieu of the actual job situation is to become personally involved in some actual problems which intramural directors encounter frequently.

The following cases are actual problems collected from various schools and intramural directors. The problems selected are in the areas of facility use, eligibility rules, protest procedure, maintenance and repair, and employee relations. The value in working through a case is dependent on involving the students in determining the solution or the direction in problem solving. This democratic approach assists the students in developing an appreciation of problem solving and administrative concern. Autocractic decisions tend to be far less acceptable than shared views and discussion which involve students. Direction toward solving aproblem may be regarded as problem solving.

Place yourself, as you may well be, as the intramural director in each of these cases. What would you have done? Was the problem handled well? Was the way in which the problem was solved efficient? Were students or employees helped or hindered in developing mature attitudes by the decisions and the way in which they were reached?

There are a number of Questions for Consideration listed for each case. These are not all of the questions that might be necessary to discuss the case intelligently. They are to be used only as a starting point, if questions do not naturally occur to the readers.

It is suggested that complete freedom be allowed among the class. The instructor, acting only as an arbitrator and consultant when his advice is requested, will help his students more rapidly begin independent thinking and questioning and problem solving.

There is no need to determine one fixed, unanimous solution to each case. The value, again, is in the thought processes and discussion which the student experiences during the case situation.

## Case 1

### COORDINATION OF AREA USE

On January 5, 1959, a student group reserved the gymnasium area for a dance. The reservation was made through the intramural director. The director then notified the varsity coach using that area on the same day. The varsity coach used the area, which was a small portion of a large intramural area, regularly.

On the day preceding the dance, February 4, the men bringing in racks and tables for coats, found the area strewn with mats and other varsity equipment. "Instead of rolling up the mats or pushing them aside, the men walked directly over the mats, soiling them with their street shoes," said the director.

The varsity coach went immediately to the intramural director and demanded to know why he was not notified just prior to the dance. The coach said it was the responsibility of the building administrator, the intramural director, to have the custodians roll up the mats.

The intramural director felt it was the coach's responsibility since he had been notified well in advance. The coach said, "The same thing happened last year. How long is this going to go on? Somebody should pay for having those mats cleaned."

*Questions for Consideration*

1. Should a student group be allowed to use the gymnasium floor for dances?
2. Would you have notified the coach a second time just before the dance?
3. Who should have removed the mats before the workmen came in?
4. How can the workmen be educated about mats?
5. Could anything have been done previous to the incident that might have prevented the recurrence?
6. Who would you have pay for cleaning the mats?

## Case 2

### PLEDGE-RULE PROBLEM

Our major problem this winter and spring has been with a number of houses who have recruited outstanding intramural athletes. These students have not been either pledges or actives of any fraternity. However, some of the houses have been using these students under a "social membership." This consists of a boy merely paying the social dues for that season, which allows him to participate in dances, dinners, outings, as well as other social functions. Because the all-year point contest is very close this year, a number of the houses have taken advantage of the fact that it isn't covered by the rules.

The above is a statement made by the intramural director.

In the *Intramural Handbook*, there is no rule that would indicate that a student must be an active or a pledge to represent a fraternity or sorority. There had been no apparent problem before as the houses had been using only those students who were either actives or pledges.

The director accepted the protest by Able Fraternity against Beta Fraternity concerning the use of the social members, and presented it to the intramural committee. (When a member of the committee is involved in a case, he is automatically relieved of his duties for that case.) The committee, composed of two seniors, two juniors, one sophomore, and one freshman, rejected the protest on the grounds that there was "no rule that would disqualify anyone from playing for a fraternity." The committee further stated, however, that a rule limiting fraternities to only pledges and actives on their teams should be placed on the book for the next year.

*Questions for Consideration*

1. Is a committee of students capable of making fair and intelligent judgments concerning their fellow students?
2. Why do you suppose there had been no rule covering that particular situation in the *Intramural Handbook?*
3. If the intent of the rule was to bar nonmembers, would it not be a violation to use such players?
4. What position would you, as director, take in this case?
5. Does the fact that the time for the all-year contest was close have any bearing on the case?
6. Should there be all-year point systems?

## Case 3

## RULE PROTEST

On October 6, 1958, a formal protest was filed by team Baker to the effect that although the official had made a ruling that followed the intramural rules, the rules were incomplete:

Intramural Sports Department

Dear Sir:

This communication is a formal protest against a decision which was made by the officials during a touch football game between Baker House and Candy House at 4:20 p.m. on October 6, 1958. The circumstances are as follows:

The "B" teams of Baker and Candy had battled to a scoreless tie during regulation playing time. The ball was then brought to the mid-field stripe by the referee, and the procedure which follows a tie game was carried out. The referee tossed a coin; Candy won the toss and elected to start the series of downs by defending the west goal. Baker began the series with a pass play. On this play, a fifteen-yard penalty for pushing was assessed to the Candy team. This penalty put the ball fifteen yards within Candy's territory. Immediately after the penalty was paced off, Candy took the offensive position but failed to gain any ground. Baker again took the ball and they were held without gain. On Candy's next chance, they gained twelve yards on a pass play, leaving the ball about two or three yards in the Candy side of the mid-field stripe. It was at this time that the disputed play took place. The ball was snapped to the Baker fullback, who faded back to pass. As he released the ball, the Candy end broke through and blocked the pass before it passed the scrimmage line. The ball fell to rest nearly four yards into the Baker side of the mid-field stripe. The referee ruled that the ball was dead where it had landed rather than returning it to the line of scrimmage, which was two yards into the Candy team zone. He based his decision on rule 14, which states: "a forward pass which ends behind the line is treated as a lateral." Following the decision, the Candy team ran a sneak play to end the overtime period. The victory was then awarded to them.

There are several factors which lead the members of the Baker team to believe that this rule did not apply to the circumstances which arose in yesterday's game. The pass in the game yesterday was an attempted forward pass with a downfield receiver. The above-stated rule is in existence to make pass, repass plays, and other such maneuvers possible, not to impose a penalty upon a team which had a pass attempt blocked, as was the case yesterday. Upon making a protest to the field supervisor, rule 14 was once used as a reference point for the decision. We of Baker House feel that under the before-mentioned circumstances, the Candy House team should not have been awarded the yardage necessary for the victory nor should they have been awarded the victory. We hope the Intramural Sports Department will give this matter the attention we feel it deserves.

Signed, Baker House Intramural Manager

The rules specify that each team will have a certain number of alternate downs to settle a tie game. The team that is in the opponent's territory at the end of the downs will be the winner. Play starts at mid field.

It was established that the protest was true in every respect.

The director rejected the protest, after meeting with the officials. He felt that "even though the rule did not cover the situation, it would not be fair to the other team that had been playing under the rule to change the decision."

The rule was changed for the remainder of the games that year to give adequate coverage to the situation. "The fact that we admitted the error of the intramural rule, but at the same time explained the problem of replaying the game, seemed to satisfy the protesting fraternity," the director stated.

*Questions for Consideration*

1. If the rule was inadequate and, in fact, decided the game, should the game have been replayed?
2. Do you think the frankness of the director in admitting an error was significant?
4. How far must a director go in rectifying his own error?
5. Would you have commended or corrected the official for the way in which he handled the situation?

## Case 4

### PRIORITY OF GROUND WORK

Just recently, we had a break in the water main under one of our softball diamonds. This was not reported to us by the groundsmen, who must have known about it because they were in the area. Our ground crew works directly for the athletic department. We found out about it only when the teams arrived to play. They reported that the water covered the diamond. The intramural supervisor and I went over, and I declared the field unplayable. The supervisor laid out a temporary diamond nearby.

The above is a statement by the intramural director.

The director further stated: "The groundsmen must not have even cared that we had games scheduled, or they would have notified us so we could contact the teams and reschedule the games.

"Each year, it is the same old problem. It doesn't make any difference if we tell them a week or a a month ahead of time as to when we are going to start our program. We still, in some cases, have to delay the start of the games a day or two. Either they haven't lined the fields or done whatever work is necessary for the playing of the games," declared the director.

The director is sure the athletic ground crew has the attitude that "it's just for the intramural office." The intramural director said he had talked a number of times with the athletic director, and all he got was agreement about the problem but no action. The intramural director decided the only way he could get help was to ask for more money to hire student help to do the work.

*Questions for Consideration*

1. Are there any means of solving a problem to which your immediate superior is indifferent?
2. What would happen if the intramural director let the problem go and just started the games if and when the fields were ready?
3. How might the athletic director be impressed with the importance of providing good ground crew service?
4. How might the ground crew be educated to the need for better service?
5. Is it better to do the work yourself or insist that the ground crew do the work?
6. Could the attitude of the intramural director affect the reaction of the ground crew foreman and crew?

## Case 5

## EMPLOYEE RELATIONS

Connie Johnson, sports supervisor for women's basketball competition, supervises thirty-two men and women basketball officials. Court assignments and work schedules are made two days in advance and available to officials in the central office. Two officials failed to check in the office, call in, or be present for three separate work assignments.

After the first error in responsibility, Connie contacted each of the officials and notified them of the scheduling procedures and requested cooperation and compliance. On the second occasion, she notified the director, and the director contacted each of the student officials. Each student assured the director that they were interested in retaining their work and would be present. After the third absence, Connie and the director decided not to further assign these students to games.

*Questions for Consideration*

1. Are written or unwritten guidelines helpful for student employees, the officials, and the sports supervisor?
2. Should student work experiences parallel actual work experience outside of the school or university?
3. Should the sports supervisor have assumed all responsibility for the students' work record and solving the problem?
4. Were there any other possible approaches to encourage the officials to assume their work responsibility?
5. Would these same students be employed again in the same capacity or another?

**References**

*Book*

Zeigler, E. F. *The Administration of Physical Education and Athletics—The Case Method Approach.* New York: Prentice-Hall, Inc., 1959.

# Competitive Units in Intramurals

## FACTORS TO CONSIDER

The designation of leagues and teams is an important phase in the success of an intramural program. Considerable differences in the intramural competitive units may exist because of varying local conditions. Age, interest, group connection, school enrollment, and facilities are some factors which should be taken into consideration when establishing competitive units for intramurals. Other considerations include group loyalty, social outcomes, and equality of competition.

Competition with established rivalry should be dealt with cautiously. A new intramural director may not be aware of intense rivalries that need no further stimulation. This is sometimes true of geographic areas and established community groups. It may be advisable for the new director to try to use the units that form naturally into competitive groups. At the secondary school level, the natural units consist of grades or classes, homerooms, and physical education classes or sections.

Intramural directors must be alert to allow for expansion and modification of the types and number of units as the school develops in size. Community development may also call for some further alterations in long-existing unit groupings.

## COMPETITIVE UNITS AT THE SECONDARY SCHOOL LEVEL

There are numerous possibilities for competitive units at the secondary school level. A few of these are considered under the appropriate heading in the discussion which follows.

### Grades Or Classes

In small schools, grades or classes often serve as the only competitive units. In larger schools, the classes usually have too many members to provide activity for enough students if only one team represents the class. When this situation arises, several teams can be selected from each class and given appropriate names for identification. When the grade or class unit of competition is used, the range of difference in ages should be taken into consideration. For example, ninth grade students should not be expected to compete against twelfth-grade students in vigorous team activities. They may be allowed to do so in certain other types of activities if there is provision made for equalization of competition by some sort of handicap for the younger age group.

### Homerooms

This unit is the most practical and popular team group in use at the present time. Most schools have homerooms as a part of the administrative plan. The number of boys and girls in each room is usually adequate to provide enough members for the various teams. Homeroom team spirit is easily stimulated because of the frequent homeroom meetings. Also, administrative problems may be minimized when homerooms are used as competitive units. The homeroom period is a good time to announce information about intramural activities and also serves as a good place to elect a manager to organize intramural teams.

### Physical Education Classses Or Sections

The physical education class or section is an ideal place to stimulate interest in intramural activities. Many individual and some team events may be organized in this period. The physical education class should not become a period of intramural contests. However, the organization of teams might well be started here. Any intramural team activity conducted during the class period should be of the type that includes large numbers of participants. This practice will reduce the number of students who must stand on the sidelines and wait their turn. Students not participating may be used as scorers, officials, timers, and for other tasks connected with the contest.

Individual activities, such as sports skills, can be conducted easily in the physical education class period. The students who have become proficient in the particular skill may engage in activities such as free throwing, softball target pitching, golf putting, archery, football target pass, as well as numerous others.

The number of days spent for intramural competition may be governed by the number of days per week that the physical education class is held. If there are five days a week of physical education, one day might profitably be set aside for intramural activity. If only two or three days are scheduled for physical education, the intramural activity might be held every other week.

### Residential And Geographical Locations

This plan is practical when there are well-defined sections of the community. When the elementary schools are used as a nucleus, there is residential grouping of the students attending the same school. Where this includes a wide range of social and socioeconomic areas, this plan may cause problems rather than be of help in alleviating them.

### Church Groups

Many communities have formed teams to represent the various churches of the communities. To carry this plan into the school situation would be unnecessary and could be unwise. Local policies must be carefully studied so that no undue rivalry is created among the church groups and religious faiths.

### Arbitrary Units

It is sometimes necessary to arrange teams arbitrarily by designating leaders and giving them a team name. Colors, college names, big league baseball teams, and other team names are popular. This type of unit can be used during free periods and Saturdays, when organized play is not scheduled.

### Independent Or "Choose Up" Teams

There should perhaps be some provision made for the students to select teams and compete in an independent league. A disadvantage of this type of unit, when it is used exclusively, is that some students might not be chosen for a team.

### Established Organizations

It does not seem a wise policy to expect such groups as the Young Men's Christian Association, Girl Scouts, Boy Scouts, and others to serve as competitive intramural units. These groups have been founded on other interests and they usually do not wish to devote time and effort as a group to large-scale intramural activities.

Some groups within the school, such as the photography club, home economics club, and the like, may wish to engage in competition against each other in a form of intramural activity. This type of unit most often occurs on a challenge basis because these groups are generally formed to fill the needs of students in a specific type of extra-class activity.

## COMPETITIVE UNITS AT THE COLLEGE LEVEL

In most colleges, competitive units consist predominately of dormitories, fraternities, and independents. Interclass, which was the first kind of organized intramural competition, has diminished among the larger colleges because of increased enrollments. Some small colleges may still use this system, but it has the same disadvantages in college as in high school. Other less widely used competitive units include the colleges within a university, departments, military units, and established organizations.

### Dormitories

Practically all colleges have dormitories or college living quarters for a great number of students. The dormitories are usually divided into sections and precincts that include from thirty to sixty students. A precinct is a natural grouping, and competition can be conducted within each dormitory, with the winning teams or individuals meeting for the dormitory championship. In some activities, such as swimming, track, tennis, and golf, it seems to be more practical to have one team made up of players from all of the precincts representing the entire dormitory. In sports like touch football, basketball and softball, each precinct may have one or more teams. An intramural athletic representative can be elected by the dormitory residents to act as the liasion between the intramural office and the precinct intramural managers. All information can be distributed to the athletic representative who, in turn, delivers it to the precinct teams. Residents of the dormitory should be allowed to compete with independent teams if they cannot be served by the dormitory teams.

### Fraternities

Fraternity intramural competition is natural, and it is a greater problem to avoid overemphasis than it is to create interest. Fraternities usually have athletic representatives and an administrative organization similar to the dormitories. If the number of members becomes too great for one team, additional leagues may be formed. Another method of giving all fraternity personnel the opportunity to participate is to allow fraternity members to play on teams in the independent leagues.

By tradition, fraternities have been the most dominant groups in the college intramural program. The director should plan the program so that all students have equal opportunity to participate whether or not they belong to a fraternal group.

### Independents

Independent students are those individuals not affiliated with a fraternity and not living in college housing. Some colleges have more difficulty securing independent participation than others. When the independent teams are offered the same opportunity to play the same sports as the dormitories and fraternities there is a great deal of interest among these unorganized groups. The most difficult task among the independent groups is that of communication. The independent groups have no common housing, and each team has its own manager. Meetings, newspaper notices, and posters are some of the best ways to let the independent teams know about the activities offered.

One method of organizing the independent teams is to use a ward system that divides the college community into separate areas. Everyone living in a certain area plays on that particular team. Intramural representatives are selected, and they help disseminate the necessary information.

In some schools, any student may play in the independent league regardless of his affiliation. Through this procedure, students are allowed a greater range of choice as to team membership. All-year point systems can be arranged for independent teams which increase the likelihood of the teams remaining together throughout the year.

## Open-Independents

Clerical, maintenance, administrative, and faculty personnel may be organized into a league for team or tournament play in individual sports. An open-independent league for non-students allows an opportunity to serve all members of the campus community. Special arrangements can be made for courtesy play in addition to the regular student league play. This extension of service would incorporate all leagues as much as possible. If specific eligibility or administrative guidelines exist preventing full competition among leagues, an exception could be made informally with team participants.

## Other Campus Groups

Any group that has a large enough student body to sustain competition may be organized. The number and type of campus groups varies at each university. If sufficient interest is evident and time and facilities permit, each of these different groups can be provided with intramural activities. Their organization is similar to the other leagues with athletic representatives and team divisions.

## Questions for discussion

1. What are some of the possible units of competition for intramurals at the secondary school level? What are the advantages and disadvantages of each?
2. Which competitive units adapt themselves naturally at the secondary school level?
3. In organizing competitive units for intramurals at the secondary school level, to what extent should the loyalty factor be considered? The social factor? The competitive factor?
4. What are some of the possible units of competition for intramurals at the college and university level? What are the advantages and disadvantages of each?
5. Should intramural competitive experience be made available to faculty and other staff members in the college or university? Should there be priorities for students, faculty, and staff?

## References

*Books*

Hughes, William L., and Williams, Jessie F. *Sports: Their Organization and Administration,* New York: A. S. Barnes and Company, 1944 pp. 85-87.

Lockhart, Aileene, and Mott, Jane A. *Teams and Tournaments.* Fond du Lac, Wisconsin: National Sports Equipment Company, 1954.

Mueller, Pat, and Mitchell, Elmer D. *Intramural Sports.* New York: The Ronald Press Company, 1960.

Voltmer, Edward F., and Esslinger, Arthur A. *The Organization and Administration of Physical Education,* 3rd edition, chapter 9. New York: Appleton-Century-Crofts, Inc., 1958.

*Periodicals*

DeNike, Howard R. "How Good Is Your Intramural Sports Program?" *The Physical Educator,* October 1965.

Schurer, W. W. "High School Intramural Programs." *Scholastic Coach,* October 1952.

# Classification of Students for Intramural Competition

## PURPOSE AND NEED FOR CLASSIFICATION

The primary purpose of classification is to equalize competition. There have been various tests constructed for the purpose of determining athletic ability. These tests are primarily concerned with isolated motor skills that make up the different sports. As yet, no single test has been devised that will determine just how good an athlete a boy or girl will become. Distinction can be made between the poor player and the superior player. This distinction can be made by most physical education teachers or coaches after short observation of the individual.

The difficult elements to measure in testing for athletic ability are the split-second mental reactions, emotional control, and competitive spirit and determination. Few of these intangibles can be measured with much degree of accuracy by any of the tests so far designed. The best that can be done by the various classification indices is to group the students by age, height, and weight. This grouping is based upon the logical assumption that those students of similar proportions and age in junior and senior high school will have somewhat similar ability.

The director should make every effort to keep intramural competition equalized. No intramural program can hope to achieve its objectives if the leagues are dominated by the larger, older, and more skilled students. The director should arrange enough different league levels so that each group will have equal opportunity to achieve recognition. This can be accomplished when students are properly classified according to ability.

## CLASSIFICATION FOR GROUP COMPETITION

Some intramural directors will not find time to classify each student by one of the various formulas that use a combination of age, height, and weight. It is very important, however, that each director be aware of the reasons for such plans, and that he have a knowledge of how to classify by these methods. Differences in age and size can be controlled in an intramural program to a certain extent by putting various rules and regulations into effect. The most practical division is by grades, and this is one of the reasons why homerooms within a grade make desirable competitive units. Usually there is only a one or two-year age difference between the students in any given grade. The weight and height ranges will not be excessive except for a few individuals within each grade. It is possible to allow certain team competition between grades only one year apart—such as ninth and tenth, tenth and eleventh, and eleventh and twelfth. Sports such as touch football and wrestling are better confined to the separate grades. These are the sports in which the action is most likely to cause injuries because of differences in size and maturity if competition takes place between the grade levels.

The choosing of teams by the students does not insure that there will be complete equality among the groups competing. If there is no administrative plan that makes students eligible for certain teams, many of the boys and girls with less ability might never be chosen to participate. The leaders who are selecting teams from natural groupings will logically attempt to secure the most proficient intramural players. If a team is confined to a room or part of a grade, the team will have to be comprised of those students available.

It is possible to rate various teams on ability, if time and facilities permit. One practical method is to hold preliminary competition before the actual league play is started. Teams that are undefeated in these games may be placed in one league. Other teams can be placed in various leagues on the basis of their ability in terms of the preliminary play.

## CLASSIFICATION FOR INDIVIDUAL COMPETITION

Classification for individual competition may be considered from a different point of view. As mentioned in Unit VI, there may be freshmen students who will be able to compete in some activities on an equal basis with seniors. In such sports as golf, tennis, badminton, and the like, there is little chance of injury from body contact and size is not necessarily a great advantage. Nevertheless, the more mature students are likely to be more proficient. Consequently, it seems best to plan different classes of leagues as in the group activities. However, if participants of different age and size compete, the competition can be operated on a handicap basis. As a director gets to know the abilities of the participants in specific activities, he can arrive at reasonable handicaps for various kinds of competition. For example, when he has an idea of the times and distances of different participants for a track meet, he can use this information to handicap the meet and equalize competition.

In some sports such as bowling and golf, methods of handicapping are generally recommended procedure in operating leagues. Bowling leagues are often operated on the basis of a certain percentage of the difference of the average scores of teams or individuals. Beginning bowlers usually have leagues handicapped on the basis of seventy-five percent of the difference of the averages. For example, if the average of Team A is 750 pins and the average of Team B is 650 pins, the handicap for Team B would be 75 pins. This figure is derived by taking 75 percent of 100, which is the difference in the averages.

The same general idea applies to handicapping for golf matches. One system of golf handicapping is based upon the five best-to-par scores. If the difference between the total of the five best scores and the total of the five pars is zero through three, above or below, there is no handicap. When the difference is four through nine, the handicap is one; ten through fifteen, the handicap is two; sixteen through twenty-one, the handicap is three, etc.

## PHYSICAL EXAMINATIONS AND CLASSIFICATION

When possible, it is highly recommended that intramural participants be given a physical examination to determine their health status for competition. The final authority in determining the health status of the student will be the school physician or the family physican, or the family physician only, depending upon the school policy.

In general, the physical examination should separate those students who are (1) sufficiently physically developed to compete in all activities; (2) those who are physically able to compete but have minor correctable defects; (3) those who have major correctable defects who, after corrections have been made, may be able to take part in all activities; and (4) those with permanent major handicaps who might suffer injury or further physical disability if allowed to participate in intramural activities.

It is possible that a restricted program for the last two groups may be developed. Care should be taken not to create a "duffer's" club or team, either in the restricted program or in any classification of a league, for those who have less skill. No student wants to be identified by name or implication with the "have-nots." Interest of the less skilled student will be much greater if the teams and leagues in which he or she participates receive the same recognition as others.

### Questions for discussion

1. In what way do the so-called natural units of competition adapt themselves to classification of students?
2. Can we always rely on the natural units as a means of equalizing competition in intramural sports at the secondary school level?
3. When is it not advisable to rely entirely on the natural units for equalized competition in intramural sports at the secondary school level?
4. What is meant by classifying students for competition on the basis of size and maturity?
5. What are some of the limitations in using size and maturity as a basis for classifying students for competition?
6. What are the possibilities in using skills tests as a basis for classifying students for competition in certain specific activities?
7. To what extent should health examinations be used to classify students for intramural competition?

### Assignments

1. Consult the references, and select a measure of size and maturity. (An example of a measure of size and maturity is McCloy's Classification Index). On the basis of the measure of size and maturity that you select, equate the following junior high school boys into three groups for competition in an intramural activity.

| Name | Age | Height | Weight |
|------|-----|--------|--------|
| Frank | 13 | 54 | 80 |
| Jim | 13 | 65 | 104 |
| Joe | 12 | 58 | 80 |
| George | 12 | 69 | 128 |
| John | 14 | 60 | 133 |
| Jack | 15 | 54 | 86 |
| Bill | 14 | 64 | 124 |
| Tom | 13 | 60 | 83 |
| Fred | 15 | 58 | 130 |
| Don | 14 | 57 | 93 |
| Ted | 12 | 58 | 110 |
| Pete | 13 | 54 | 79 |
| Ed | 12 | 56 | 95 |
| Mike | 13 | 57 | 101 |
| Pat | 15 | 58 | 122 |

2. Select a skills test from the literature, and write a brief description of how you would use this test to equate a group for competition in the specific activity. Consult the periodical references in this Unit in selecting your skills test.

3. Devise a system of preliminary competition that would result in leagues or tournaments between teams or individuals of approximately equal ability.

### References

*Books*

Clarke, H. Harrison. *The Application of Measurement to Health and Physical Education,* 3rd edition, chapter 14. New York: Prentice-Hall, Inc., 1959.

Mathews, Donald K. *Measurement in Physical Education,* chapter 7. Philadelphia: W. B. Saunders Company, 1958.

McCloy, Charles H., and Young, Norma Dorothy. *Tests and Measurements in Health and Physical Education*, 3rd edition, chapter 30. New York: Appleton-Century-Crofts, Inc.

*Periodicals*

Clarke, H. Harrison, and Bonisteel, H. A. "Equalizing the Abilities of Intramural Teams in a Small High School." *Research Quarterly of the AAHPER*, vol. 6, March 1935.

Cox, Walter A., et al. "Equating Opponents in Junior High School Activities." *Research Quarterly of the AAHPER*, vol. 6, March 1935.

Hill, Eugene. "Factors Involved in Selecting Units of Competition for Intramural Activities." *National Intramural Association Proceedings*, 1966.

Lockhart, A., and Mott, J. A. "An Experiment in Homogeneous Grouping and Its Effect on Achievement in Sports Fundamentals." *Research Quarterly of the AAHPER*, vol. 22, March 1951.

Miller, K. D. "Classification of College Men by the Wetzel Grid." *Research Quarterly of the AAHPER*, vol. 22, March 1951.

Stansbury, E. "Classification of Boys for Physical Education." *Research Quarterly of the AAHPER*, vol. 12, October 1941.

Wear, C. L., "Test for Classification." *Research Quarterly of the AAHPER*, vol. 2, May 1940.

Whitney, Frank. "Junior High System for Sport Participation." *Scholastic Coach*, October 1958.

# Facilities and
# Time Allotment for Intramurals

## BASIC CONSIDERATIONS OF FACILITIES AND TIME ALLOTMENT

All school administrators are confronted with the problem of time and space allotment. The intramural director who can satisfactorily organize and coordinate his space and facilities for intramural activities will have solved one of the greatest problems. To the new intramural director the problem of facilities and time allotment seems an insurmountable one. At first glance, it will appear that every area is scheduled for every hour.

The director must take into account the fact that the facilities and participants must be available at the same time. Consequently, an overall view of the extra-class activities must be considered. A faculty meeting—where the director may present what he is trying to do—is a good method of gaining cooperation. Before the meeting, the director can contact each faculty sponsor of the various student clubs and other local school groups that use the same facilities. This type of planning tends to reduce the friction that is brought about by the problem of the use of various facilities at specified times. Since an intramural program is a service for all students, most faculty members are inclined to cooperate with any reasonable plan.

To aid in organizing the time and facilities available for the intramural program, a calendar of events and master schedule should be devised. Not only does this system allow the director to plan his own activities for the year, but it also allows him to arrange for the rest of the school's programs that involve the use of physical education facilities. Such information as the dates of school plays, varsity contests, dances, meetings, and other events that may conflict with intramural activities should be recorded. The director can then schedule the intramural contests on days and at times when there are no conflicts. This does not imply that the intramural program should be allotted only the time that is left by the other groups. Many of the dates may be arranged in conjunction with other faculty sponsors.

In setting up his own schedule, the director should also have a calendar of events indicating the intramural activities for the entire year. The director's calendar can be used to note such information as the date when publicity should be started for an event, when awards and equipment should be ordered, and when team rosters should be prepared. Figure 4 shows an intramural director's calendar for the first four-week period of a school year.

One of the greatest conflicts in terms of facilities is with the varsity athletic program. Because of the similarity of activity in both programs, the same facilities are often in demand at the same time. It is important to consider here both programs from an educational point of view. What should be the primary consideration for varsity teams? Is the end goal the winning of games? Or is the end goal the development of the individual through participation at the varsity level? Is it educationally sound to provide facilities only for the members of a varsity squad? Is it educationally sound to provide the areas only for the numerous intramural teams? The best policy obviously lies between the two ex-

| | | | | | |
|---|---|---|---|---|---|
| Publicity for Touch Football Starts<br><br>September<br>15 Monday | Publicity for Tennis Starts<br><br><br>16 Tuesday | Order Fall Awards<br><br><br>17 Wednesday | 18 Thursday | 19 Friday | 20 Saturday |
| Publicity for Football Pass Starts<br><br><br>22 Monday | Noon Hour Program<br><br><br><br>23 Tuesday | <br><br><br><br>24 Wednesday | <br><br><br><br>25 Thursday | Deadline for Touch Football and Tennis Entries<br><br>26 Friday | 27 Saturday |
| Touch Football Starts 4 P.M.<br><br><br>29 Monday | Tennis Tourney Starts<br><br><br>30 Tuesday | <br><br>October<br>1 Wednesday | Marching Band Practice<br><br>2 Thursday | Varsity Football 3:30 P.M.<br><br>3 Friday | 4 Saturday |
| Football Pass Starts 3 P.M.<br><br>6 Monday | Order Basketball and Winter Awards<br><br>7 Tuesday | Noon Hour Film<br><br><br>8 Wednesday | <br><br><br>9 Thursday | <br><br><br>10 Friday | 11 Saturday |

**Figure 4.** Sample of an Intramural Director's Calendar for a Four-Week Period

tremes. Both programs have value alone. Both programs have added value when they exist together. Many more students may actually participate on intramural teams than on varsity teams. It is entirely justifiable then, when no other time and facilities are available, to divide the facilities between the two programs. If the value of participation in varsity sports is the true goal, then allowing intramural use of facilities one or two days of the week certainly falls within the realm of educational objectives.

The season of the year must be given consideration along with the geographical location of the school. In areas where there is cold and inclement weather during the winter months, the facilities always become more limited because of the necessity of holding most of the activities indoors. The program is generally divided into fall, winter, and spring activities. In areas of the country where the climate is mild throughout the year, there is much more latitude for scheduling the year's activities. An intramural director should not let himself become bound by tradition in scheduling winter activities. Many healthful and interesting activities can be conducted on the community's hills, ponds, and lakes.

To alleviate conflicts, the intramural sports seasons can be changed. For example, softball can be played in the fall, with touch football in the spring. Basketball can also be organized during the fall and spring seasons, when the gymnasium load may be lightened. This is not altogether desirable because the intramural participant enjoys playing the same sport that is also being played by the varsity teams.

As in setting up different units for competition, it must be kept in mind that no one time will serve all of the students adequately. Different times throughout the school day, as well as afternoons and evenings, must be considered to allow many different students to participate.

## LATE AFTERNOON AFTER SCHOOL

The time available immediately after classes are over in the afternoon is a good time to carry on high school intramural activity. From the director's viewpoint, this is a good time for several reasons.

Faculty members who might help with the program would, perhaps, be much more willing to spend some time immediately after school rather than come back at night. The heating and lighting costs are small because the plant is already in operation. A very important factor is that the custodian is still on duty and available for services. Moreover, the director is on hand to start the activities with little waste of time.

From the student standpoint, the afternoon activity is welcome after attending classes all day. The students are at the building and have only to go to the locker room, change clothes, and be ready to play. There will be some students who work at this time and others who must travel by bus. No one time can ever be found that will serve all of the students. Other times, that will be discussed later, should be provided to enable these students to participate. If the schedule is well planned in advance, many of the working students can arrange their schedules to coincide with one or two afternoons of activity. For the program that has demonstrated its value, it may be possible to provide extra buses, or an alternate bus schedule on certain days, to allow students who must travel to join the activity.

Parents generally favor afternoon activities, primarily because the students do not have to go to and from school during the evening hours. In the larger communities especially, parents are sometimes reluctant to allow their children to walk to school and back at night.

Interesting intramural activity available at the school after school hours will reduce the number of students who have nothing to do and help to channel their time into healthful and wholesome recreative pursuits.

One of the major difficulties in having an afternoon intramural program is the use of the facilities at this time for varsity practice. Fall and spring seasons are not as much of a problem as the winter season because outdoor areas are usually available. If time is not made available by dividing the days with the varsity teams, it is sometimes possible to use the period immediately preceding varsity practice. Intramural contests can be scheduled on those days when varsity games are played during the week. Varsity teams generally do not practice on the day of a game, which leaves the facilities open for intramural use. The same situation prevails when the varsity team is playing away from home. Every minute of time should be explored by the intramural director for possible use. Arrangements should be made with all of the members of the coaching staff so that the intramural director is notified when time is available in any area.

Afternoons can be used most effectively for intramural activity by the smaller colleges. In large colleges and universities, however, with the many different class schedules for students, it is not the best time for intramural competition. Most colleges have classes until five o'clock in the afternoon and a dinner hour from about 5:30 P.M. to 6:30 P.M. Tournaments in individual sports, with students making their own playing dates, are possible during the afternoon period. Team activities, however, have not always proved to be too successful when conducted at this time.

## EVENINGS

It is difficult to hold high school intramural activities at night. The students who are scheduled to take part have to arrange transportation to and from school. As mentioned previously, parents in most communities do not want their children out on school nights. The director has an added problem of custodial services. Also, it is more difficult to secure the aid of other faculty members for supervision at night. Another problem is the conflict with adult recreation programs which are sometimes conducted in the evening.

Varsity games, dances, and community functions that take place in the evenings sometimes conflict with the scheduling of many of the intramural activities. Perhaps the best use of evenings is made by planning a number of special programs "sports' nights" and "parents' night." By planning the program well in advance, other activities can be avoided, and plans can be made by students and their parents to attend. Programs of this type are very useful in creating interest for the intramural program among the adults of the community. Otherwise, many parents might never get a chance to see the physical education facilities of the local schools. Activities can be planned for father-son and mother-daughter participants as well as for competition among the students.

Some localities have lighted outdoor facilities and artifical turf or have such facilities in the planning stage. The additional expenditure for developing indoor or outdoor athletic facilities is much more acceptable to the community if many students will benefit from increased court or field space. When facilities are shared, better attitudes are developed toward varsity events for the few; and actual, full utilization warrants the investment and development. It is important to consider intramurals, athletics, and physical education in the development of facilities as well as on the actual scheduling of already existing facilities.

When there is no other available time to conduct intramural activities, it is justifiable to plan an evening program. Careful planning must be done to safeguard the students and prevent an excess of night activities that would not be commensurate with student needs.

At the college level, it has been found that evenings are a very practical time to conduct the bulk of the intramural program. Touch football under lights in the fall season, and basketball during the winter, can take place after the dinner hour. In early spring, it is difficult to play a full softball game between 5:30 p.m. and darkness. In May and June, the days are long enough to play two five-inning games, starting at 5:30 p.m. Fields for touch football can easily be changed to softball fields to utilize exterior lights during the best seasons for play.

To avoid unnecessary conflicts with the many extra-class activities offered at most colleges, regular days may be scheduled for certain groups. Monday and Wednesday, dormitory games may be scheduled throughout the year. Independent games can be played on Tuesday nights, with fraternities competing on Thursday. Friday night is not a popular intramural night in colleges because of the many social events and the fact that a great number of students go home on weekends.

## NOON HOUR

The use that can be made of the noon hour varies greatly at each school. Differences in scheduling create lunch hours ranging from one-half hour to a full hour or more. Most school situations require the establishment of some type of organized activity for the students during this time. In some schools, if there is not a planned noon program, numerous problems are created when hundreds of students are released for the lunch period. The students who buy their lunch at the cafeteria or bring their lunch from home usually finish eating in fifteen or twenty minutes. As a result, it is important to provide some sort of program for these students.

Various types of activities may be conducted, but there are some basic policies which should be followed in any noon-hour program. Adequate time must be allowed for the participants to eat their lunch. Although high school students do not appear to suffer serious effects from eating and competing in physical activity, it may be difficult to justify to parents a program that encourages rapid eating, with strenuous competition immediately following. A solution to this problem, if highly competitive sports are conducted during the noon hour, is to allow the students to eat after the activity.

Time to change clothes and to take a cleansing shower also must be provided if active games are to be played. No physical educator can justify students competing in street clothing and then going directly to classrooms without taking showers. Strenuous opposition may be voiced by the classroom teachers. This practice is unhealthful, unsanitary, and extremely unpleasant for both students and teachers who must endure the perspiring players for the next hour. If adequate time for eating and taking showers is possible, games such as basketball, touch football, and other active sports may be satisfactorily conducted. This is especially important if a great number of students are unable to stay after school because of bus transportation or jobs.

In some cases, a study hour or free period is scheduled following the noon hour. This arrangement makes possible adequate time for almost any type of activity. More value can be gained, however, by use of activities adaptable to corecreation and social situations. This period could be a popular time for students of both sexes to participate together in corecreative activities. After eating lunch, groups of students can move to the gymnasium, and other rooms and play areas, to play table tennis, checkers, shuffleboard, dart games, volleyball, basketball, and other enjoyable activities.

Other programs include listening to tapes and records, library activity, movies (showing physical activity films—games, Olympics, World Series, high school game films), ethnic dancing, or viewing demonstrations of particular sports, dance, or martial arts. In some high schools, the various clubs of the school assume the responsibility for planning the noon-hour programs for each week. The director and students are bound only by their imaginations in designing the noon-hour program. Many schools now have split-shift lunch hours, with two or three scheduled periods for lunch. A combination of physically active games or swims could be arranged, with a non-activity program as well. If the teacher who is responsibile for the noon-hour activities makes arrangements to eat lunch early, he or she can be on hand throughout the entire period. This should relieve other teachers from supervision duties in other areas of the school. A system of rotation, whereby one teacher takes charge for a number of days and then is relieved, should spread the responsibility more equally. This supervision is sometimes assigned by contracted agreement through faculty associations in lieu of class assignment or for extra pay.

The director should have the program planned in advance so that the activities do not depend upon the ability and enthusiasm of the particular teacher on duty. If teaching loads can be adjusted, one teacher may supervise the noon hour every day. It is best to have a teacher volunteer for this assignment rather than imposing the job on one who does not have an interest in the program.

## DURING THE SCHOOL DAY

Some of the times available for intramurals during the school day include: (1) in the morning just before the first class; (2) during free or study hours; (3) during the physical education period; and (4) during a regular activity period.

Students who travel by bus often arrive early before school starts. Activities similar to those provided at the noon hour can successfully take up that time which might otherwise be wasted in sitting around waiting for the first class.

During the day, several study periods will be scheduled. Sometimes arrangements can be made with teachers to allow students who have prepared their lessons to go to the gymnasium for informal activity. Using the study hours for intramural activity is dependent upon the facilities being free at the same time. Informal recreative and corecreative activities can be used with success during these periods, provided there is adequate supervision.

The physical education class may be used for limited intramural competition. The primary purpose of the class is to provide learning experiences in physical education. If contests are held, activities that include large numbers of students should be used. As mentioned in a previous unit, teams may be organized in physical education classes for competition at other times. If there are five periods of physical education during the week, one day may be profitably used for intramural activities. It was indicated in Unit VI that intramural competion can stimulate the interest of the students in physical education classes. This interest can be increased also by allowing students to represent their physical education classes in individual sports tournaments. Points can be given for each match won, and a mythical class winner can be determined. It is doubtful if credit toward the physical education mark should be given for intramural participation in regular physical education classes. No pressure should be brought to bear on students to make the program merely an extension of the required class.

In some high schools, it is common practice to schedule one period daily for an activity period. As a rule, all club and extra-class activities take place at this time. In some cases, this activity period is used for intramural participation, and, in most instances, it has proved to be quite successful.

## SPECIAL ACTIVITY DAYS

An intramural program that has proved its worth usually gains the cooperation of the entire staff. Principals will often cooperate in arranging half-day recesses which will allow the entire student body to participate in a well-planned program. Many different activities may be planned, both inside and outside the school. Teachers can be assigned to various areas to keep score and to supervise the contests. Any number of skills, contests, and games may be arranged in a county fair or carnival fashion. Groups of students representing classes can move from area to area, accumulating points toward the day's championships.

This type of program must be well planned to allow all groups to compete in all activities. Timing is important to keep interest up in each area. The approximate time of each event, with brief instructions as to procedure and the location of each succeeding event, should be clearly defined. The special activity day is a very good way to create interest in the regular intramular program offered each day.

## SATURDAYS AND VACATION PERIODS

Saturdays and vacation periods can be utilized to supplement the community recreation program. Some students who are unable to participate during the week may have Saturday mornings free. Efficient use of such large community investments as school plants should encourage the use of the facilities on Saturdays and certain holidays and vacation periods.

Outdoor facilities can be placed in full operation all day long if sufficient supervision is provided to insure equal use by all groups. Tennis courts and other individual games areas should be made available on days the school is not in session.

One of the main problems comes in arranging for supervision of the various facilities during the off days. If the school administration is convinced of the value of opening the play areas, adjustments in teaching loads may be made. The person in charge on Saturday mornings might be relieved from classes on Friday afternoons. A rotation plan, similar to assignment of other school duties, may be arranged in order to divide the extra time equally among all staff members. If such an arrangement cannot be effected, additional salary should be obtained for the provision of supervision of intramural activities while the school is not in session

### Questions for discussion

1. What is the relationship between facilities and time allotment for intramurals?
2. What are the advantages and disadvantages of having the program take place after school?
3. What are the advantages and disadvantages of having the program take place in the evening?
4. What are the advantages and disadvantages of having the program take place during the noon hour?
5. Under what circumstances is it possible to conduct an intramural program on Saturdays, holidays, before school in the morning, during school hours, during vacation periods?

### Assignments

1. Your high school principal has asked you to conduct an intramural basketball program for boys at the noon hour during the winter months. The noon-hour period is sixty minutes in length. On the day that a team plays, its members will be allowed ten extra minutes to get to the first-period class following the noon hour. Make up a time chart showing how you would divide the time for this program. Be sure to make allowance for playing time, dressing, eating, and other factors.

2. Draw up a calendar of events for one semester—showing the different activities offered, when they would start, and how long they would run. Explain your reasons for your method of setting up the program.

### References

*Books*

Kleindienst, Viola, and Weston, Arthur. *Intramural and Recreation Programs for Schools and Colleges.* New York: Appleton-Century-Crofts, 1964.

Mueller, Pat, and Mitchell, Elmer D. *Intramural Sports.* New York: The Ronald Press Company, 1960.

*Periodicals*

*Athletic Institute,* "Intramurals for Elementary School Children," "Intramurals for Junior High School," "Intramurals for Senior High School," 1964.

Chellman, John. "Competition in The Intramural Program." *Journal of Health, Physical Education and Recreation,* May 1959.

# Activities in the Intramural Program

## BASIC CONSIDERATIONS

The selection of activities for the intramural program is dependent upon a number of basic factors. Some of these factors include needs of students, interests of students, facilities and equipment available, and the amount of time available. It is the primary purpose of this unit to consider the contributions that certain activities can provide. In addition, some practical suggestions for administering the activities are discussed. The rules of the various activities may be obtained in any guidebook or rules pamphlet distributed by sporting goods stores and companies. Official rules for girls' sports are published by the Division for Girls' and Women's Sports; rules are available in sporting goods stores or may be obtained through the A.A.H.P.E.R. offices in Washington, D.C. Time and space are not devoted in this unit to the reproduction of the various rules. Rule modifications are suggested to better fit intramural situations.

If the educational objectives of the program are to be adequately met, thought must be given to the selection of the activities which will make up the intramural program. It is obvious that the type and amount of facilities will, to a considerable extent, govern the kinds of activities that can be conducted. However, the director must show originality and resourcefulness in devising new play areas and in making game modifications that will allow maximum use of every square foot of space.

## POPULARITY OF ACTIVITIES

Tradition is likely to have a decided influence upon the popularity of various intramural activities. If the adults of the community engage in and promote certain recreative activities, these same activities are likely to be popular with the youth of that community. The cost involved is an important factor, both to the participant and to the intramural director. An activity that requires expensive personal equipment or costly team equipment may be popular with only a select number of students. The sports that can be conducted in the standard facilities present in most schools will no doubt have greater participation than those sports that are more expensive to conduct and need special facilities. However, some activities that call for monetary investment may be very popular and participated in for a longer period of time because of greater interest and time spent, as well as money invested.

## VALUE OF ACTIVITIES

The intramural director must take other factors into consideration in addition to student interest and popularity of activities. This is a very important matter, because the director must intelligently bridge the gap between what the students want to do and what will best assist them in developing new activity attitudes and skills which provide for regular participation and a lifetime sports or activity interest. It would certainly be unwise to plan a program based entirely on what the director decided were the most valuable activities. Without the proper orientation and education, the students might be inclined to ignore what may be new to them and continue what they had always done.

This does not imply that these two views are far apart and never coincide. On the contrary, it is the job of the director to attempt to provide students with those activities that they are interested in, and at the same time, broaden student interest and familiarity with other activities that are of value for current enjoyment and future use.

## CRITERIA FOR THE SELECTION OF ACTIVITIES

The intramural director should attempt to apply certain valid criteria to the selection of activities. The following generalized list of criteria is intended for use as a guide for specific situations.

1. Does the activity contribute to the physical needs of students?
2. Does the activity contribute to the social needs of students?
3. Does the activity contribute to the emotional needs of students?
4. Does the activity contribute to the intellectual needs of students?
5. Does the activity contribute to the recreative needs of students?
6. Is the activity conducted in such a way that it will promote the health and safety of students?
7. Is the activity planned in such a way that all students have equal opportunity to participate?
8. Is the activity interesting and appealing to a majority of students?

It is doubtful that any one single activity will satisfactorily meet all of these criteria for all students. Consequently, a variety of team and individual competitive sports, as well as individual and and group non-competitive activities, are recommended for a well-balanced program.

With the facilities available, equipment needed, popularity of the activity, and the inherent values of the activity to guide him, the intramural director must do his best to provide as many activities as possible that will meet the established criteria. With sound reasons for providing certain activities for the students, the director can more easily convince the school and community of the need for additional facilities and play areas.

## TYPES OF ACTIVITIES

There is almost an unlimited range of activities which can be used in the intramural program. These various activities may be classified on the basis of team, individual, competitive, non-competitive, recreative, seasonal, and the like. The activities discussed on the following pages by no means cover the total range of intramural possibilities. On the other hand, a few of the popular activities are discussed, and certain interesting aspects of them are presented. Although many of the activities are indicated by seasons, this does not imply that the director is obligated to operate an activity in a specific season. On the contrary, it may be necessary to operate certain activities out of the regular season in order to make proper adaptation to the local situation.

## FALL ACTIVITIES

### Archery

This activity has grown tremendously in some sections of the country through the impetus of the fall bow-and-arrow hunting season. Bowman's clubs are easily formed and they help to provide for continued interest. If the director can obtain one or two archery sets and target faces, running records can be kept for two or three varying distances. Care must be exercised in the selection of the site for the archery range and in the provision of proper supervision. Six arrows make up an end. One end can be shot at each distance. This is a very good corecreative activity.

## Track and Field

Availability of an open track and field for leisure running, jogging, and jumping is becoming increasingly in demand. Boys and girls enjoy individual or small group running workouts. Indoor and outdoor tracks can be made easily available to the school and community for continued enjoyment in running.

## Soccer

This activity is fast becoming one of the more popular intramural sports. Any reasonably sized field should prove satisfactory for a playing area. The only other requirements are two-by-four goal posts and a ball.

## Touch Football

This is the most popular outdoor fall intramural sport for boys and girls at all grade levels from the junior high school through college. Much unfavorable comment has arisen from time to time because of the injuries reported from the game. A very successful method of reducing injuries is to orient the players and officials thoroughly concerning the situation in which injuries are likely to take place and the rules concerning those situations. An open type of game, with unlimited forward passes and four downs in which to score, tends to reduce much heavy line blocking. Penalties, such as loss of the ball for diving on a fumble and one-half the distance to the goal line for illegal blocks, will also discourage those acts that may cause injury. With four downs allowed for the length of the field, no measuring equipment is needed. The game is high scoring because of the many combinations possible, with all players eligible to pass and receive. Seven players, with unlimited substitutions, for a field of eighty by forty yards, is very satisfactory.

## Turkey Trot

This activity is merely a cross-country type of run, with a few novelties and social aspects added. It should be conducted within two weeks of Thanksgiving to add to the holiday spirit. The running course should be situated in the vicinity of the school grounds so that students and faculty may view the entire race. Both individual and team competition is possible, with the first four men who finish for a team making up the team score. Girls' clubs and organizations can be encouraged to sponsor the various boys' teams by making color sashes and having the team run under the name of the girls' group.

Girls may wish to be included in the field of competition and run separate teams or mixed teams. Live turkeys and other fowl, awarded as prizes, create much interest and spirit. The distance for high school competition should be no longer than one mile.

If a large number of entries is anticipated, a finish chute should be erected to insure that correct placing positions are maintained. Cards with numbers from one on up can be given to each student as he finishes in each position. In this way, the scorers can quickly record the individual's name and place. At least four practice runs, as well as a physical examination, should be required for each participant.

# WINTER INDOOR ACTIVITIES

## Badminton

A few inexpensive rackets and nets can make this sport possible in any school. Temporary lines can be made with chalk or tape, and each player can buy one or two shuttlecocks. If the loser is allowed to keep the used shuttlecock and the winner the new, then no player need purchase more than the original shuttlecock.

## Basketball

Basketball is the most popular intramural activity in practically every locality. Most schools have the necessary facilities to provide for this activity. Very few rules changes, other than the reduction of playing time, is necessary to adapt the game for intramural play. It is a difficult game to officiate well, and care should be taken in the selection and training of officials. Teams should not be permitted to play more than one game daily.

### Basketball Free Throw

Certain days may be scheduled as the time for participation in the free-throw contest. Any number of shots may be designated. Each participant can report to an intramural worker at the basket where his throws are to be taken. His record should be recorded, and at the end of the specified time, the individual and team with the highest total is declared the winner. Any number of members of a group may represent their team, with the highest four or five contestants' scores taken as the team total.

### Basketball Golf

Various spots are set up at varying positions and distances from the basket. The player attempts to make a successful shot at each "hole." Running records posted by the basket can be kept for a number of weeks to determine the season's winner.

### Bowling

The growth of the community recreation leagues has made this activity a national winter pastime. Arrangements can usually be made with community bowling alleys for special rates and certain times for the intramural leagues. Corecreative bowling is excellent and affords wholesome mixed activity. Competition can be held in single, double, team, and mixed events.

### Boxing

Boxing is a popular intramural activity in some localities. In other areas, it is not held in the highest regard. The director should very carefully determine the attitude of the school and community toward boxing before including it in the intramural program. Even in those places where boxing is popular, the utmost care must be taken to provide constant and expert supervision.

Each contestant should take part in a certain number of preliminary practices. Instruction in boxing in the physical education class is good preparation if this activity is a part of the physical education curriculum. The protective headgear is mandatory and the heavier gloves should be used. Individual rubber mouth guards should be required.

A physician should examine each boy before he is allowed to enter boxing competition. The physician should be at the ringside during all bouts, with the understanding that he has the authority to stop any bout. Careful attention should be given to the weighing-in of the contestants. No high-school boy should be allowed to move up to a heavier weight. It is also doubtful whether a boy should be allowed to train down more than five pounds below his normal weight. The three rounds should be no more than one-and one-half minutes in length, with a full minute rest between the rounds. No improvisation should be made for the ring floor. Adequate padding of at least two inches is necessary. Boxing, as an intramural sport, is more widespread at the college level than the secondary school level because colleges are more likely to have the facilities and equipment for this activity.

### Gymnastics and Tumbling

In the localities where this type of activity is popular among the adults, it is easy to create interest in an intramural gymnastic meet. The basic exercises should be used for the meet, and the instruction in gymnastics in the regular physical education classes should help to prepare those students interested in competing. If apparatus such as flying rings, horizontal bars, and parallel bars is used, the director must provide adequate safety measures for all performers. No attempt should be made to improvise this type of equipment as the contestants' welfare may be jeopardized.

### Handball

Almost every school has some flat wall space available that can be utilized for satisfactory single-wall handball. Where gloves and regulation balls are too expensive for the students, three or four pairs of gloves and a few balls can be issued by the intramural department. If this is not feasible, a modified game with tennis balls or sponge rubber balls can be substituted. Paddleball is a very exciting game that is played on the regular handball court. Paddles can be wood, fiber board, or plastic.

### Swimming

At the present time, relatively few secondary schools have swimming pools. However, often the local community Y. M. C. A. or other similar organizations have pools that can be used for intramural activity.

Entrants in swimming meets should be required to do some preliminary training and also take a physical examination. Moreover, constant supervision is essential in order to prevent tragic accidents. The events should, perhaps, be modified to a certain extent from the interscholastic or intercollegiate events to compensate for the lack of condition and training of the intramural swimmer. Splash parties, with mixed swimming, afford excellent corecreative opportunities.

## Table Tennis

Ping Pong is universally popular in all seasons. This sport is an excellent corecreative activity, and many different events can be planned for practically all grades. Singles, doubles, team, and mixed doubles tournaments are easily arranged. The industrial arts classes can make tables if money is not available for their purchase. Access to a table during off hours makes for a desirable informal activity.

## Volleyball

Proper instruction in physical education will show the students how enjoyable volleyball is when it is played correctly. Leagues can be conducted for both boys', and girls', and coed teams. Facilities are easily arranged in any gymnasium and can also be set up out-of-doors in mild climates.

## Wrestling

As in the case of boxing, extreme care must be taken to ensure proper weight matching. Usually, wrestling is more easily introduced as an intramural activity than boxing. However, it may be wise to obtain parental permission for participation in both of these sports. Physical examinations should be required as well as a minimum amount of supervised training. Regular gymnasium mats are adequate, but sanitary covering should be used to help prevent mat burns which might result in skin infections.

## WINTER OUTDOOR ACTIVITIES

Tobogganing, skating, and sledding can be incorporated into the intramural program where the weather is conducive to these activities and the facilities are available. In many cases, it has been shown that a few ice carnival days or winter sport fests are more successful than numerous scheduled events. The entire school can attend the activities, which include a great many events such as a variety of sled and toboggan races. Speed skating and mixed-couple skating are popular among the older high school students. In some communities, streets can be blocked off for an afternoon of school activity in winter sports.

## SPRING ACTIVITIES

Time is of great importance during the spring season. Many days of inclement weather must be expected, and the end of the school year allows no extension of playing time. Tournaments and leagues must be selected and planned to permit at least two weeks' leeway for schooling.

## Golf

Golf can be played on an intramural basis without the use of a full-sized golf course. A near ideal situation would be an arrangement with a nearby golf course for student play at a reduced rate during specified times. If this is not possible, a modified range can be set up on the school grounds for use at certain times. Concentric circles, drawn around a hole, can be used for hole-in-one contests. If necessary, the plastic practice ball can be used for approach and driving contests. Putting ranges or miniature golf courses are possible in almost any school situation.

If a course is available and if twosomes or foursomes are scheduled for a full round on a specific day, the names should be listed and the starting times posted so that each group can plan to be present and start on time .If the course cannot be obtained for any certain day, the paired players can be given a specified number of days in which they may get together and play the match. Medal play is perhaps the best for intramural activity because it requires only one day of play. Playing on different days might involve varying weather conditions.

## Horseshoes

Construction of horseshoe pits is possible at most schools, and the game is popular over the nation as a spring and fall activity. Quoits or rubber shoes can be used for indoor activity, but the sport is much more popular as an outdoor pastime. Both sexes can play, and competition can be planned on an individual team basis. Safety practices should be explained to all students, and the pits constructed away from congested areas. For smaller boys and girls, a lighter shoe can be obtained and the distance between the stakes reduced.

## Softball

This game is much more in demand than baseball as an intramural activity. It requires less space and equipment than regulation baseball. Spiked shoes should not be necessary; moreover, all students might not be able to purchase them. Two student officials can adequately control the game from behind the plate and on the bases. Nine or ten boys or girls may be used satisfactorily, depending upon the local regulations. Five-inning games are satisfactory and allow more games to be scheduled each day. The slow-pitch form of softball provides many more opportunities for participants to experience certain enjoyable aspects of the game—specifically, hitting, fielding, and base running. More players are in the field, and less time is spent waiting for the pitcher to walk or strike out the batter.

## Tennis

This activity ranks with golf in carry-over value. Singles, doubles, and mixed doubles can be scheduled. To reduce the cost of the balls, the director can purchase a sufficient supply and sell them at cost to the students in the tournament. If each contestant is required to obtain one set of balls for the tournament, no one will have to have more balls because he or she wins more matches. As each match is played, only one set of balls is used. The winner takes the unused set for the next match, and the loser keeps the used set. The single elimination tournament in both singles and doubles is the most common type of competition.

## Track and Field

Participants in track events should be required to undergo training for at least one week before the meet. Distances run should be reduced from varsity events if this seems necessary, and no student should be allowed to enter more than three events, including a relay event. This procedure should not only help to prevent excessive fatigue, but it should also allow more boys and girls to participate. Team competition, as well as individual competition, can be scheduled.

A variety of novelty races, such as a three-legged race and a bag race, can be interspersed with the regular events to add more fun for the participants and spectators. One of the most important factors in the success of a meet of any kind is concerned with preliminary planning. Assistants should be assigned to each event with specific duties. Small details regarding the administration of the meet should be cared for in advance. A schedule of events—publicized and distributed at least two weeks in advance—will do much to reduce confusion at the meet.

## INFORMAL ACTIVITIES

A very popular part of any intramural program is the unscheduled or informal activity. This is merely time at which various facilities are available, and the student may draw equipment and play at his own discretion. Many of the activities are suitable for corecreative groups and as outdoor activities or club sports. Each director can select the type of an activity, in keeping with the local climate and community factor.

## SPORTS SKILLS

Experience has shown that students receive a great deal of satisfaction from trying to improve their skills in various sports. Some activities that can be used for this purpose include football pass, football place kick, basketball free throw, baseball throw for accuracy, baseball throw for distance, and golf putting.

Any skill event of this sort may be conducted by setting aside certain days and times. Contestants can sign up at the time of participation. Team scores may be obtained by counting any number of high scores as the team total.

## ACTIVITIES FOR "HANDICAPPERS"

A restricted program for those students unable to participate in the more vigorous sports may be desirable under certain conditions. Close cooperation with the school and the family physician—or the family physician alone—will usually result in the discovery of some type of activity suitable for the student with certain degrees of physical limitation. The activities listed below are a few that might be provided with a little ingenuity:

1. Archery
2. Basketball (also, wheelchair baseketball)
3. Bowling
4. Clock and basketball golf
5. Croquet
6. Quoits and horseshoes
7. Darts
8. Free throw
9. Pistol and rifle target shooting
10. Pocket billiards
11. Swimming
12. Table tennis
13. Track
14. Weightlifting

## Questions for discussion

1. What part do local conditions play in the selection of activities for the intramural program?
2. What influence do facilities have upon the selection of activities for the intramural program?
3. What influence does time allotment have upon the selection of activities for the intramural program?
4. What activities are best adapted to the fall season? The winter season? The spring season?
5. What is the place of the following types of activities in the intramural program at the secondary school and college level: Recreative activities? Vigorous team sports? Individual sports? Club sports?

## Assignments

1. Using the activities which you selected in Unit II, separate them by seasons into various classifications such as recreative activities, team sports, individual sports, and corecreative activities.

2. Make a list of the factors which actually determine the value of any given activity to the student.

## References

*Books*

Hughes, William L., and Williams, Jesse F. *Sports: Their Organization and Administration.* New York: A.S. Barnes & Company, 1944, pp. 85-87.

Irwin, Leslie W. *The Curriculum in Health and Physical Education,* 2nd edition, XI, XII, XIII. St. Louis: The C. V. Mosby Company, 1951.

Scott, Harry, *Competitive Sports in Schools and Colleges*, chapter XI. New York: Harper and Brothers, 1951.

Sharman, Jackson R. *Introduction to Physical Education*. New York: A. S. Barnes & Company 1934, pp. 160-165.

Voltmer, Edward F. and Esslinger, Arthur A. *The The Organization and Administration of Physical Education* 3rd edition, chapter 9. New York: Appleton-Century-Crofts, Inc., 1958.


*Periodicals*

*Athletic Institute*, "Intramurals for Elementary School Children," "Intramurals for Junior High School," "Intramurals for Senior High School," 1964.

Barney, Fred. "High School Intramural Sports." *National College Physical Education Association for Men Proceedings*, 1965.

Dubick, H., "Promote Intramural Wrestling." *Scholastic Coach*, Vol. 22, October 1953.

Gillingham, Evan S., Jr. "Do-It-Yourself Track Meet." *Journal of Health, Physical Education, and Recreation*, September 1964.

Harding, Carol. "Informal Drop-in Activity Program." *Journal of Health, Physical Education, and Recreation*, February 1970.

Kalla, Joseph. "School Centered Winter Sports Program." *Journal of Health, Physical Education, and Recreation*, January 1964.

Keen, P.V. "Wrestling as an Intramural Sport." *College Physical Education Association Proceedings*, 1959.

Kirk, Robert H. "Aspects of Co-Educational Intramurals." *Journal of Health, Physical Education, and Recreation*, December 1963.

Korsgaard, R. "Flag Football in the Intramural Program." *College Physical Education Association Proceedings*, 1957.

Kraus, Richard. "Which Way School Recreation." *Journal of Health, Physical Education and Recreation*, November-December 1965.

McCoy, Mary. "Fitness through Intramurals." *Journal of Health, Physical Education, and Recreation*, September 1957.

Wickstrom, R. L. "Organization of Intraclass and Interclass Track Meets." *The Physical Educator*, May 1960.

# Point Systems in Intramurals

## BASIC CONSIDERATIONS OF POINT SYSTEMS

The number and variety of point systems for both groups and individuals are perhaps as numerous as the number of schools that use such plans. As in the many other phases of intramural programs, practices and policies regarding point systems differ in each locality. There are, however, some fundamentals that should be considered in order to provide for fairness, adequate coverage, and achievement of planned objectives.

It is not imperative that point systems be used in intramural programs. In fact, an unwisely weighted point system may create many of the problems the director is attempting to eliminate. It is more important that a wide variety of activities be provided. If both individual and group activities are liberally distributed throughout the year, the majority of the students who participate will be reached. However, many students in college and in high school need just a little more incentive to induce them to take the time and effort to join the fun. It is these students that may be reached by the use of point systems.

## GROUP SCORING SYSTEM

It has been found, through experience, that group point systems of any value influence an intramural program in a number of ways. The program may be motivated, and more interest may be generated by the teams and groups. There is likely to be more continuity from season to season, with the teams making plans to participate on a long-range basis. Because of the increased interest in the existing teams, more teams are apt to be formed by students reacting to the enthusiasm. Intramural directors can stimulate the students to widen the choice of sports in which they participate by awarding group points for many different activities. Groups that sponsor teams rapidly learn that they must field a team in each activity to keep abreast of the other teams in the league.

There are certain precautions that should be taken when planning a group scoring system. All teams must have an equal opportunity to gain the points offered. Each must have competition in the same number and type of activities. In weighting the points, care must be taken to avoid causing the participants to lose the value of the play for the sake of gaining the points. Regulations should be provided to prevent teams from entering strenuous sports for which they are unprepared physically, for the sole purpose of gaining additional points. For example, students might be limited to participation on one team in any one sport. This prevents individuals from participating in more than one activity a day. It also insures more participation because teams will have to use more different players rather than a select few. The use of a point system may put a great deal of pressure on the competing groups. The director must make the decision as to how much emphasis should be placed on accumulating the most points. To keep the competitive spirit within bounds, the weighting of the points in favor of participation over winning is important.

Points can be given for entry of a team and the playing of a number of games. Also, points can be given for participation in all of the games scheduled and for each game won. In some intramural point systems, teams are penalized for forfeiting scheduled games. When the purpose of the program is participation, it may be justifiable to take participation points away from the groups that do not appear at the scheduled time.

The reason for giving a varying number of points for different sports is primarily based on two factors. These factors are concerned with the number of students participating in the activity and the length of time or the number of participations by the student. For example, touch football should perhaps receive more points than tennis because from twelve to twenty students would participate in each touch football game. The competition would perhaps run for approximately six or eight weeks, allowing each contestant to play five or six games. A tennis match includes two or four players, with three or four matches being played by the winner and runner-up.

It is questionable whether the terms "major" and "minor" sports should be used to define the various sports activities. All sports have value for the individual; and, as there are little or no gate receipts in connection with intramural sports, the connotation is erroneous. This should be taken into consideration in the awarding of points.

## INDIVIDUAL SCORING SYSTEM

An individual scoring system can be coordinated with a group plan in many ways. An individual plan is justified because it allows for recognition of the entire student body. In other words, a student is not required to compete on an organized team in order to receive recognition. At the same time, more group participation is stimulated because individuals may receive credit for both types of activities. Another advantage in applying an individual point system is concerned with its adaptability for including all of the intramural activities provided by the school.

Credit for non-competitive activities, such as hiking, cycling, skating, boating, fishing, and hunting, may be given on an individual basis. The time spent at the activity and achievement in the activity can be used as a basis for point scoring.

As in the group scoring system, there are precautions which should be taken to prevent unsatisfactory conditions that might develop because of the decision to accumulate points. If a plan is devised for the year to determine an all-intramural champion, it is obvious that any students interested are very likely to enter all possible events. If precautions are not taken, students might spend an undue amount of time in intramurals only for the purpose of gaining points. For this reason, there should be intelligent scheduling of the activities. Spacing the various events with ample time between each different activity automatically tends to reduce the chance of a student attempting to engage in too many activities.

Another important problem is the awarding of points to organizations, homerooms, or independent teams for participation by individuals. If this plan is used, some individuals may be requested by friends to enter competition for which they may not be fit or in which they have no skill or interest. In sports like cross country and wrestling, it is particularly important that no student enter merely to win some points for his particular group.

Intramurals should be based in so far as possible on voluntary participation. Intramural objectives may be lost if the school requires the student to participate, or if the student is more or less coerced to enter by his organization. Each director must plan his point system to fit the local conditions. Application of certain basic principles previously mentioned should insure an adequate point system.

### Questions for discussion

  1. What are some of the advantages of point systems in intramurals?
  2. What are some of the disadvantages of point systems in intramurals?

3. With regard to point systems, what is meant by group scoring?
4. With regard to point systems, what is meant by individual scoring?
5. At which level are point systems most important—the secondary school level or the college level? How do you support your decision?

## Residence Hall Point System

These systems award points to all participating teams. More points are earned for participation than for winning. Teams do not have to be the champions to earn points. The residence halls accumulating the most points throughout the year are their leagues' all-sports champions.

|  |  | Participation | 75 | 45 |
|---|---|---|---|---|
|  |  | Performance |  |  |
|  | Handball, Golf | First | 45 | 25 |
| Basketball | Badminton | Second | 35 | 20 |
| Bowling | Paddleball | Third | 30 | 16 |
| Volleyball | Swimming | Fourth | 25 | 14 |
| Softball | Table Tennis | Fifth | 20 | 12 |
| Touch Football | Tennis, Track | Sixth | 15 | 10 |

## Fraternity, Sorority and Independent Point Scoring System

Organizations accumulating the greatest points throughout the year are their leagues' all-sports champions.

Fraternity and sorority and independent teams that forfeit more than one game will lose their participation points.

In single-elimination tournaments, place points will be earned only from the first full round (a round with no byes). Place points will not be earned or awarded in the event of forfeits or circumstances that enable a team to reach the finals without winning a match. Forfeiting teams will lose tie positions.

|  |  | Participation | 75 | 45 |
|---|---|---|---|---|
|  |  | Performance |  |  |
|  | Handball, Golf | First | 30 | 25 |
| Basketball | Badminton | Second | 25 | 20 |
| Bowling | Paddleball | Third | 20 | 16 |
| Volleyball | Swimming | Fourth | 15 | 14 |
| Touch Football | Table Tennis | Fifth | 10 | 12 |
| Softball | Tennis, Track | Sixth | 5 | 10 |
|  |  | League Winner | 45 |  |
|  |  | League Runner-up | 35 |  |

Figure 5. Michigan State University Intramural Scoring Plan for Team and Individual Activities

## Assignments

1. Devise a point system for seven individual activities. Justify your different evaluations of the activities.

2. Devise a point system for five team activities. Justify your different evaluations of the activities.

3. On the basis of the analysis of the school in Unit III and the competitive units selected in Unit VI, devise a point system which you feel would be adaptable for the particular situation.

## References

*Books*

Hughes, William L., and Williams, Jesse F. *Sports: Their Organization and Administration.* New York: A. S. Barnes & Company, 1944, pp. 338-346.

Leavitt, Norma and Price, Hartley D. *Intramural and Recreational Sports for High School and College,* 2nd edition, chapter 8. New York: The Ronald Press Company, 1958.

Means, Louis E. *Intramurals: Their Organization and Administration,* Englewood Cliffs, New Jersey: Prentice Hall, Inc. 1963.

*Periodicals*

Curry, Nancy. "What's The Point of Points?" *National Intramural Association Proceedings,* 1972.

Pederson, Eldon E. "The Intramural Point System." *National Intramural Association Proceedings,* 1963.

# Awards and Incentives in Intramurals

## JUSTIFICATION AND POLICY

The opportunity to experience satisfaction and earn recognition for effort and achievement is one of the greatest forces in America. In all types of endeavor, young and old alike earn recognition for their skill and perseverance. The pleasure and satisfaction that people derive from accomplishing a certain goal oftentimes is a sufficient incentive to insure completion of the task. For those persons, an award is the final gesture of a series of satisfactions derived from the activity itself. These people would have participated in the activity regardless of whether or not awards had been offered. It is believed that our educational process today is guiding more and more students along this path by encouraging them to participate in wholesome activity primarily for the enjoyment and challenge that the activity may provide. However, it is true that more zest and challenge is involved with the opportunity to earn an award of some kind.

There are some educators who are of the opinion that awards are so closely related to rewards that they should not be given for achievement purposes. Perhaps one should consider that awards are not given as favors or rewards for doing something for somebody else. Awards are earned by the individual's own effort and determination and are recognition for these qualities.

Awards should be used as the means to an end rather than the end itself. From this point of view, awards for intramural participation and achievement appear justified. If, in the effort to gain an award, the student experiences the values attributed to intramurals, he or she certainly benefits from the participation. In this connection, the director must be careful to plan the program and the system of awards so that a minimum of students will participate only for the purpose of winning an award. The director should devise rules and regulations that will insure the student opportunities to participate in those experiences of individual and group action that are valuable. If the director relies too heavily upon expensive and ornate awards to create student interest, many of the objectives of intramurals may not be attained. If the extrinsic or material values are made the desired end, the participants may be more concerned with the award than in the manner in which they win it. As mentioned previously, the intrinsic values, or the values which are derived from the activity itself, must be the predominate factors in creating student interest.

Care should be taken to base awards on the amount of skill, time, and number of students participating. This planning follows closely that of the point systems discussed in Unit XI. Point-scoring plans can be closely related to the method of providing awards.

## FACTORS INFLUENCING VALUE OF AWARDS

To increase the interest in intramural activities that is created by awards, the director should order the awards before each season starts. When the awards are presented at the moment they are won, the students experience much greater satisfaction than if the awards are picked up at the office later. It is often possible to have an awards banquet or assembly planned later in the season.

Another method of increasing the value of awards is to have them on display. The importance of an award to an individual is very closely related to the number of people who know that he or she has earned the award. Therefore, if the award is displayed before the event and on the scene during the event, the value to the winner may be increased. It is also important that the students know how the awards are earned. In this regard, the number of points accumulated, contests won, and the amount of participation required are important factors. Charts, showing the various awards and demonstrating the manner in which they may be won, can be displayed.

The popularity of the awards can also be affected by the ease in which they may be won. If so many awards are offered that it takes little or no effort or skill to win one, the value of the award may be decreased. There may be little satisfaction derived from winning an award if it is not difficult enough to achieve. On the other hand, the awards should not be too difficult to earn. If only the very top individuals who are near the varsity level of performance are able to win awards, the average intramural participant may lose hope of ever earning one. The new director might try plans that have worked at other similar institutions until he is able to modify and devise the plan that is best for his particular school.

## DISTINCTION BETWEEN VARSITY AND INTRAMURAL AWARDS

Awards in the form of sweaters, letters, and emblems have traditionally been provided for varsity athletes. The student who is able to satisfactorily represent the school on a varsity team deserves the award that is offered. High schools in most states must conform to state high school regulations that limit the financial value of these awards. Most individual intramural awards will not approach this financial limit, but, obviously, regulations must be considered. Almost without exception, the varsity athlete devotes much more time and effort to his activity than does the intramural participant. The varsity athlete may also sacrifice many more personal desires for the benefit of the team. For these reasons intramural awards should not be so similar as to be confused with varsity awards.

## CLASSIFICATION OF GROUPS

The different groups from which teams and individuals are drawn will determine to some extent the types of awards which should be provided. There are certain permanent groups in all schools that have a common basis for their organizations. Groups such as homerooms and clubs can be awarded trophies, plaques, or cups. These organizations have a place to display the award where all members can enjoy it. These permanent groups are easily adapted to all-year or all-intramural awards because the group remains the same, although there may be different members on different teams throughout the year. In many cases, individual awards are not given to the members of teams of such permanent groups. However, if it is financially possible, each member of the team might also receive an individual award.

Temporary groups are those which consist of teams formed from physical education classes, study halls, and the like. These groups are less united than the permanent groups because they are not likely to have a regular base of operations. However, if they meet for some common activity during the week, a sense of unity can be established and teams organized for that particular season. At the end of the term or year, the unit is dispersed and new groups are organized. Team trophies can be presented to these groups if there is available space to display such awards in the gymnasium or corridor. Individual awards should also be given to the members of the teams formed from temporary groups.

Independent teams that are organized by enterprising individuals generally have no common meeting place. Consequently, there may be little need for a team trophy for these groups because the unit usually dissolves after the season is ended. However, individual awards can be presented to members of these teams. In cases where it seems desirable to have the same type of trophy for the independent teams as for the other groups, this trophy should be on display somewhere in the school, with the appropriate engraving on the name plate. The names of the winning teams can be placed under the heading, with the year it was won.

All of the team awards should be similar so that there is little or no distinction between the groups. Each student should have the opportunity to earn the same awards, regardless of the group he or she is representing.

The director should attempt to plan the individual activities throughout the year so that too many tournaments in the same sport will not be conducted. Rules which eliminate the previous winners may serve the purpose of encouraging more entries and greater distribution of awards.

It is customary to give awards to winning teams and second-place teams. In individual events such as swimming, track and gymnastics, individual awards can be given to the first, second, and third-place winners in each event. In events such as sports skills, individual awards can be given as far down as the first five if the number of participants warrants it.

Trophies can be awarded to the team that accumulates the most points for the entire year. It is possible to have a number of all-intramural champions. If different grade levels and leagues have different sports and do not compete from league to league, there can be an all-year champion for each group. This same plan can be arranged on an individual basis if a point scoring system is used.

## SOURCES OF AWARDS

The most successful and practical plan for the awarding of trophies is on the rotation basis. Any number of years may be set up as the requirement for retiring the trophy. Trophies and cups of any size are expensive. If there is any conflict between the purchase of awards and the purchase of equipment, the latter must take precedence. For this reason, the awards must be placed on the most economical plan. Trophies can be designed in any manner which enables a director to obtain a few good trophies with large areas for the engraving of team names. In this way, no team nor group keeps the award. The group that wins the competition in a certain year has its name engraved on the name plate and keeps the trophy until the following year. The cost of awards is then reduced to individual awards and engraving. Units might be permitted to purchase smaller replicas of the trophy through the intramural office, if they desire.

It is possible, in many schools, to make very satisfactory awards in the industrial arts department. This is a commendable practice since it tends to integrate intramurals with another department of the school as well as reduce the cost of awards.

Another source of awards is from local commerical and service organizations. However, the director must exercise caution when accepting this type of assistance from commercial concerns. There should be assurance that the awards are being given in the best interests of the participants and that they are not to be exploited in any way. The director should refrain from canvassing local community groups for awards and other aid. Most of these local groups are called upon for support in many community and school projects, and repeated requests may cause a certain amount of resentment.

## TYPES OF AWARDS

Team awards, in both high school and college, generally consist of trophies, cups, or plaques. Any of these may be obtained in any size, at varying prices, through local sporting goods stores or jewelry stores. Plaques are easily made in the industrial arts department and are very good for display in corridors and on gymnasium walls. Names of winning teams and individuals can be lettered on the plaques, along with the sport and the year of the competition.

Photographs of teams and individuals also make very satisfactory awards. Student photography clubs can be involved as a special project or activity.

Individual awards generally consist of medals, emblems, banners, pennants, ribbons, pins, and certificates. Almost any awards catalog will list these various types. Most companies can make up an item with some distinguishing feature of the school. Many of these items can be made in the school in the departments of industrial arts, home economics, or printing. If a medal is designed and used year after year, the cost is reduced because the same die may be used with different sport insets. The certificate is a practical award and can be used successfully as an immediate award at the conclusion of an event. It can also be used to identify the individual at a later date if a more permanent award is to be issued. Colored ribbon can be purchased in rolls, cut to shape, and a typewriter can be used to print the necessary information on the glossy side.

Individual records in time and distance for specific events may be kept yearly, along with and for the purpose of compiling cumulative all-school records. The records can be kept current and displayed in a public hall area or display center. Students and alumni value this traditional record keeping, and a natural base is established for the student to compete against the current standing record. This type of public record keeping is actually regarded as a meaningful award by students, and other material awards such as trophies, medals, and letters can be used but are not necessary. The public index of records or the use of photographs with the records formulate a challenge to participation.

In some instances, the intramural managers who serve the program over a specified period of time are given awards for achievement and service. This is a desirable practice, and it is highly recommended that it be followed when possible.

A very adequate intramural program can be conducted without any awards. The same program, however, can be stimulated by the proper use of inexpensive awards that are intelligently distributed.

## Questions for discussion

1. What is meant by the intrinsic and extrinsic values derived from intramural sports?
2. What is the difference between "rewards" and "awards"?
3. What is the place of manager's awards in intramurals?
4. What are some ways of obtaining awards on an inexpensive basis?
5. What are some of the types of awards given in intramurals at the secondary school level? At the college level?
6. What is the place of awards offered by commerical groups, such as newspapers, industry, or radio stations, in intramural sports?

## Assignments

1. Devise an award plan for a high-school program that includes two leagues, five team activities, and ten individual activities. Name the types of awards and number given in each case.

2. Devise an original award for an intramural sport in the form of a certificate or plaque. Draw your specifications for the award in the space provided.

## References

*Books*

Irwin, Leslie W. *The Curriculum in Health and Physical Education,* 2nd edition, chapters XI, XII, XIII. St. Louis: The C.V. Mosby Company, 1951.

Leavitt, Norma, and Price, Hartley D. *Intramural and Recreational Sports for High School and College,* chapter 8. New York: The Ronald Press Company, 1958.

Mueller, Pat, and Mitchell, Elmer D. *Intramural Sports.* New York: The Ronald Press Company, 1960.

Voltmer, Edward F. and Esslinger, Arthur A. *The Organization and Administration of Physical Education,* 3rd edition, chapter 9. New York: Appleton-Century-Crofts, Inc., 1958.


*Periodicals*

Ali, Edward. "Motivation Through Recognition." *The Physical Educator,* May 1967.

*Athletic Institute.* "Intramurals for Elementary School Children." "Intramurals for Junior High School," "Intramurals for Senior High School," 1964.

Boycheff, Kooman. "Promotion of Intramural Sports Through Photography." *National Intramural Association Proceedings,* 1962.

Kaywood, R.. "Awards in the College Intramural Program." *Journal of Health, Physical Education and Recreation,* October 1950.

Kelsey, William J. "Trophies for Intramural Participation." *Scholastic Coach,* April 1965.

Unruh, Dan. "Awards, New Ideas, and Promotional Techniques." *National Intramural Association Proceedings,* 1966.

# Rules and
# Regulations for Intramurals

## BASIC CONSIDERATIONS

In developing the policies by which the intramural program is to be governed, factors concerned with the aim and spirit of intramural rules and regulations should be kept in mind. It is impractical and difficult to devise rules that will entirely cover every phase of the program. Therefore, the participants must be oriented and educated concerning the aim of the rules and the purposes of the intramural program.

There are certain natural phases into which regulations for an intramural program can be divided. Rules of the various sports sometimes need to be modified to fit intramural activity with regard to safety, space, facilities, and time allotment. Also, definite rules should be devised to control and protect intramural participants with respect to participation, eligibility, protests, postponements, and forfeits.

The basis for modifying rules of certain sports has been covered, in part, in Unit X. It should, perhaps, be emphasized that one of the most important considerations for modifying the rules of sports is concerned with the safety and welfare of the participants. Other considerations that must be taken into account are space and facilities and the amount of time required to complete an activity. Care must be taken in modifying any game rules to keep the essential elements of the game, with optimum play intact. This unit is primarily concerned with those regulations having to do with the participation of the students in the program.

The purposes of the intramural program should be reviewed with regard to the aim of the participation rules. It has been stated previously that the provision of enjoyable activity, in which accepted values are inherent for all students, is a primary purpose of the intramural program. This is particulary important for those students who are not able to participate in the varsity athletic program. It is questionable whether those students who derive the benefits from varsity training, conditioning, coaching, and practice should be allowed to participate in those particular intramural sports in which these factors would be an advantage. When the students understand the value in protecting the intramural level for the intramural participant, they will no doubt support the rules which restrict the varsity athlete. The varsity athlete is provided with one level of activity, and the intramural participant should also be provided with another level of activity.

## AWARD WINNERS

The general consensus of opinion holds that varsity letter winners should not be permitted to participate in sports in which they have earned their letter. Generally, this is not a great problem because the letter winner is usually playing on the varsity squad during that particular season. Since there is a direct advantage gained, and since for an athlete in-season time is so limited, the restriction of the athlete is accomplished by practical consideration, more than by specific regulations.

In many cases, it may also be wise to consider a policy that varsity letter winners in any sport should also be restricted from certain other intramural activities as well as in the same sport in which they are a letter winner. It has been found, in many instances, that most students capable of earning varsity letters in any sport are exceptional intramural athletes. This is due, in part, to natural ability, coordination, and size, and, in part, to the superior coaching, practice, conditioning, and training habits that are direct results of varsity participation. This carry-over from the varsity sports is especially apparent in such intramural sports as track, touch football, basketball, and softball. If the varsity athletes are allowed to participate in these activities, it is possible that they will tend to dominate the activities. For each position on an intramural team filled by a varsity athlete, an intramural level player will be left out. He then will, perhaps, be unable to participate satisfactorily at any level. The thought is that since the varsity athlete is already receiving the benefits of coaching and other values, it seems only just to provide the same experiences for other students. Because it is difficult to separate the varsity sports with regard to value and experience received, it may be better to restrict all varsity award winners from those intramural sports that are also played on the varsity level.

The more recreative types of activities, such as swimming, bowling, golf, and tennis, might be open to the varsity letter winner of other sports. These are sports calling for certain specific skills that may not be inherent in some of the varsity team sports. It also encourages those players to learn activities that will perhaps be of more use to them after school years.

Another method of reducing the advantage of varsity letter winners in the intramural program is to arbitrarily select groups of two or three to organize teams in the various sports. This procedure tends to equalize the teams, and if the athletes are properly oriented, they can bring about closer relations between the varsity teams and the student body. This type of arrangement should, perhaps, be conducted either before or after the regular varsity season.

To provide intramural activity for the varsity letter winner and still protect the intramural participant, special open or unlimited tournaments or leagues can be organized. Teams in these leagues can be made up of any student enrolled in school. The varsity players enjoy this type of league as the competition is usually close and the quality of play is high. At the college level, freshmen athletes who receive numerals should probably be required to wait one year before they compete in that particular intramural sport. If the player does not go out for the sport in his or her sophomore year, and the coach feels that the student's ability is not of varsity standard, the player could be allowed to compete in those intramural activities in which he won numerals on an intercollegiate basis.

## VARSITY SQUAD MEMBERS AND RESERVES

There are a number of problems connected with those students listed on the various athletic squads who may not be in the category of letter winners. Any plan will be difficult to operate unless there is complete cooperation between the varsity coaches and the intramural director. In borderline cases, the opinion of the coach concerned should be obtained. The coach is in a position to judge the ability of a player, the length of time he has been on the squad, and whether it would be unfair to other intramural players to allow the questioned player to participate.

Many schools do not allow any squad member to participate in any intramural activities during the season. There is a problem of time involved, but it may be advisable to allow squad members to participate in those recreative activities in which there is no obvious advantage. Included here are such activities as bowling, swimming, handball, and the like. In some instances, varsity athletes are involved in sports seasons throughout the entire year. These students will have little or no opportunity to learn the valuable carry-over activities if they are restricted during the varsity season.

Rules should be devised to cover those students who drop from the varsity squad or are cut after a period of time. There are obvious problems connected with these individuals. For example, if a squad member drops from the track squad the day before an intramural track meet, he has a decided advantage over the intramural participant by virtue of his training and coaching. A specified waiting period should help to reduce this problem because the student has then had time to think ahead about his decision rather than being persuaded at the last minute to run for the intramural team.

In team sports, it may be especially important to observe a waiting period. Also, a definite rule seems necessary with regard to the length of time a student may be on a squad and still enter intramural competition. There are a number of ways to determine this period of time, depending upon the local situation. Some schools set the date at four weeks after the starting date. If a player is still listed and has a squad locker at the start of the fifth week of practice, the player is no longer eligible for intramurals. Other schools work out an arrangement with the coaches so that those players who are released from the squad on the first or second cut are eligible. Sometimes the coaches designate the first game as the final date that a player can be eliminated from the varsity squad and still play in the intramural sport. It is possible in some locations to delay the start of the intramural sport until the varsity squads are determined. Some sort of regulation should perhaps be observed in this regard because the influx of ex-varsity candidates in the middle of the intramural season might cause much dissatisfaction among players already established on the intramural teams.

## ACADEMIC REQUIREMENTS

Restriction from intramural participation on the basis of scholastic requirements does not appear justifiable. If the program has any educational value, it is doubtful that anything will be gained by depriving students with scholastic deficiencies of the chance to participate. The times when intramural activities are conducted usually do not conflict with the study time of students. Occasionally, a varsity athlete will be ineligible for varsity competition because of scholastic deficiencies. Rules for these individuals, with regard to intramural participation, should be deivsed on a fair and equitable basis. Coaches' judgments should be obtained on borderline cases of this nature.

## ROSTERS

To credit individuals with points, and to enable the intramural office to check on eligibility, all teams or organizations should be required to file a roster of their members at the start of the season. This can be done in a number of ways. Lists of the players for each sport can be required before the competition starts. The entire list of all members can be filed at the start of each season or each year. There are a number of valid reasons for requiring a roster for each activity. There is always added publicity for the sport when the rosters are called for and entry dates established. As each manager seeks players, more and more students hear of the program. Additional information can be distributed as the managers turn in the rosters. It is wise to have mimeographed forms with space for the manager's name and spaces for members of the team.

Membership in a specific group, such as class, homeroom, fraternity or club, should be decided by the rules of the school and the group. Probationary members and pledges should perhaps not be allowed to represent the group. It might be well to consider only members in good standing as eligible. Again it may be necessary to require a waiting period after full membership is attained before individuals become eligible for intramural competition. This practice discourages indiscriminate recruiting for the sole purpose of obtaining a good player for a certain event.

Independent teams must present team rosters to prevent duplication of players on other teams. Any group of individuals should be allowed to organize a team and play in an independent league. The same rules of eligibility should be required except that there need be no common bonds as in the case of a club or organization.

It must be remembered that, although administrative regulations are needed, "people are more important than materials." If a player's name is omitted from a team roster, or if the roster is not turned in exactly on time, a degree of leniency should be shown. There is obviously a limit to the amount of leeway that can be given, but every consideration possible should be made to enable the students to play. To strictly enforce administrative rules to the point of excluding participants is likely to defeat the purpose of the program.

## REGULATIONS ON INDIVIDUAL PARTICIPATION

As a general rule, students should be limited to one team in a specific activity. This reduces the chance of overexertion and allows more students to participate on the different teams. In sports such as track and swimming, it is a good policy to limit the number of events that may be entered by one individual. Three events, including a relay event, has worked successfully in some schools.

Championship play-offs should be limited to those players who have played with the team at least two times previously. This prevents the sudden acquisition of "ringers" for the final games. In individual sports, some schools restrict the previous winners for a year.

## FACTORS OF LIMITATION

There are some factors that restrict individual participation and reduce the chance for overexertion, regardless of specific rules. In the scheduling of the various activities there is bound to be some overlap, either of training periods or actual contests. The student must decide which activity he or she will enter.

The reduction of the playing space—such as two basketball floors across one varsity court—reduces the amount of exertion needed for a game. The shortened time of most contests and the shortening of the distances in such activities as track and swimming also tend to bring the sport to the intramural level of condition.

## POSTPONEMENTS

In devising the postponement regulations, the director must take into account the many activities in which students are involved. Previous planning with other faculty sponsors helps to reduce the conflicts that cause requests for postponements. Some schools follow the rule strictly, defaulting any team or player who is unable to compete at the scheduled time. Other schools set a specified time before the game as the limit by which a postponement may be requested.

Every effort should be made by the intramural director to arrange postponements if the request is caused by legitimate conflicts. Other school activities, examinations, and religious holidays should certainly be considered as legitimate reasons for postponements. The absence of a star player or the need for extra practice should not be sufficient reasons for postponing a contest. Postponements should be allowed in cases where both teams can be notified and another date can be arranged without disrupting the league play. The director must use discretion and judgment in allowing postponements so that the privilege will not be abused. It must be recognized that every game that does not take place because of conflicting events reduces the amount of participation among the students. The calendar of events discussed in Unit VIII will do much to reduce the need for postponements.

## FORFEITS

The general policy governing forfeits usually includes a time limit by which the team must appear or lose the game. In some schools, a team that arrives after the starting time is penalized a certain number of points and the game is continued from that point. Some schools require a team deposit, and each time the team is late it loses some of the deposit. If no forfeits are made, the entire deposit is returned. Participation points can also be used as an inducement to appear for every game.

It is possible to allow teams to start a game without a full team. However, to keep the game reasonably in hand, a point limit should be established. As soon as one team leads by an overwhelming number of points, the game should be called to prevent the humiliation of or injury to the other team.

When reservations are made at commercial bowling lanes, ice arenas, tennis courts, pools, or golf courses, some sort of fee should be guaranteed so that the concern does not lose money if a team does not show up at the scheduled time.

## PROTESTS

Good officiating helps to reduce the number of protests filed by intramural teams. The director should attempt to select the best officials available, train them, and then back them up completely in matters of judgment. If protests are permitted on the basis of an official's judgment, a situation may be created where there may be numerous protests because some students may never agree with decisions. Other protests stem from the use of ineligible participants—such as players who have played with other teams, are not members of the organization, or are varsity athletes.

It seems advisable to require that protests be presented in writing by a specified time after the game has been played. Investigation by the director and the protest committee can establish the validity of such protests. Proper orientation as to which varsity players are eligible and clear explanations as to the intent or spirit of the eligibility rules will help keep eligibility problems down.

Protests should be discouraged because they oftentimes contain an attitude not concomitant with the spirit of intramurals. However, the right to protest must be available to protect the teams that abide by the rules and regulations.

Specific protest procedure should be clearly delineated so the procedure itself does not become a problem. A protest form can be made on the back of the score sheet for the specific game play. The protest should be submitted within a specific time after completing the actual game. It is recommended that the maximum time be twenty-four hours and that only the protest in writing is honored. This time procedure will alleviate a postponing of games for other students or, in some instances, for members of the team affected by the protest.

If a game is protested during actual game play, the officials call official time and formally announce the game will continue under official protest of the specific team. Play continues; the game is completed; and the protest form is filed at the end of game time. It is recommended that the protesting team knows that a decision regarding the outcome of the protest will be made by a specific time. Protests can be regarded as a part of normal procedure, without students being subjected to the necessity of requesting another judgment and, therefore, being unsportsman-like or requesting an atypical procedure. Preparation and a route for any dissension is in the best interests of the participants.

---

**SUGGESTED PROTEST FORM**

Protesting Team:_____
Quarter and Time Remaining:_____
Score at Time of Protest:_____
Ball Possession at Time of Protest:_____
Situation: (For Referee's use only. Be Specific.)

_____
(Head Official)

_____
(Umpire)

_____
(Scorer)

The director, together with the protest committee, should be responsible for making decisions with regard to protests. Decisions should be made immediately upon receiving all the facts from officials, supervisor, and players. A successful practice is to ask the members of the offended team if they wish to replay the game with the ineligible player removed. It should be made clear that they are not obligated to play. In the cases where the team chooses to replay the game, a feeling of goodwill may be created among the competing teams.

## Questions for discussion

1. Who should be responsible for developing the rules and regulations for intramural sports at the secondary school level? At the college level?
2. What are the prevailing concepts with regard to scholastic eligibility and intramural sports?
3. What procedure should be followed with regard to the eligibility of lettermen and varsity squad members for intramural sports?
4. What provisions should be made for varsity players who are ineligible for varsity competition?
5. What provisions should be made with regard to the physical fitness of intramural participants?
6. Are there any situations at the secondary school level in which it would be necessary to obtain parents' consent for participation in intramurals?
7. What are some of the ways in which postponements, forfeits, and protests may be handled?
8. What are some of the problems involved in the restriction of participation in intramural sports?
9. What consideration should be given to rules for specific activities in local situations?
10. Under what circumstances is it justifiable to modify the rules and regulations for specific activities?

## Assignments

1. Write a statement of your philosophy regarding restriction of varsity squad members and award winners from specific activities in the intramural program.

2. Write the rules and penalties for all of the situations in a touch football game that are most likely to cause injury.

## References

*Books*

Hughes, William, and Williams, Jesse F. *Sports: Their Organization and Administration.* New York: A. S. Barnes and Company, 1944, pp. 326-329.

Means, Louis E. *Intramurals: Their Organization and Administration.* Englewood Cliffs, New Jersey, Prentice-Hall, Inc., 1963.

Voltmer, Edward F. and Esslinger, Arthur A. *The Organization and Administration of Physical Education,* 3rd edition, chapter 9. New York: Appleton-Century-Crofts, Inc., 1958.

Voltmer, Carl D. and Lapp, Vernon W. *The Intramural Handbook.* St. Louis: The C. V. Mosby Company, 1949, pp. 63-65.

*Periodicals*

Adams, Gary, "Eligibility Rules: Are They Enforceable?" *National Intramural Association,* 1966.

Jevert, J. A., "Guideposts for Intramural Eligibility." *National Intramural Association,* 1966.

Mueller, P. "A Positive Approach to Forfeits in the Intramural Program." *College Physical Education Association Proceedings,* 1959.

Stevens, Leonard W., "An Analysis of Eligibility Rules Used and Penalties Invoked in Twenty American Representative Colleges." *National Intramural Association Proceedings,* 1962.

# Organization for Competition and Schedule Making

## BASIC FACTORS IN PREPARATION OF SCHEDULES

In planning the competition for the various intramural sports, the director must keep one thought constantly in mind. In keeping with available facilities, time allotted, and the number of participants, a type of competition should be selected that will insure the greatest amount of playing time for the greatest number of students. If scheduling of intramural activities is completely new to the director, he should obtain the entries early in order to determine the number of teams or individual contestants. One more major factor must be taken into consideration: for activities in most climates, the weather must be taken into account when the schedule is prepared. A schedule that would finish on the last day of school might not be completed because there are usually some days during the spring season when activities may have to be curtailed because of inclement weather.

## OLYMPIC MEET STYLE

This type of competition is based on individual events in which participants may compete in a number of the various skills. As mentioned in Unit X, it is wise in intramural meets to limit the number of events in which one student may participate. These meets are usually held over a period of one or two days. This procedure allows students more opportunity to compete.

Track, swimming, and gymnastic meets require detailed planning if they are to be completed in an orderly fashion. Heat sheets, score cards, watches, tapes, and other necessary materials should be considered in preliminary planning. The order of events should be available to all contestants so that they can be prepared at the proper time. Field events in a track meet should be started before the running events because they take a longer time to complete. Arrangements at all Olympic-style events should be made to keep spectators away from contestants and judges.

## SINGLE-ELIMINATION TOURNAMENT

The single-elimination tournament is one of the quickest ways of determining a champion. The term "single-elimination" indicates that little participation is involved for at least half of the contestants. There are values in this type of tournament, however, and it may be the only possible method by which the competition can be arranged.

When the director plans any kind of tournament, he must know how many games will be necessary to complete the competition. In the single-elimination tournament, there will always be one less game than the number of teams. For example, if there are eight teams entered in a single-elimination tournament, there will be a total of seven games. Figure 6 shows an example of an eight-team, single-elimination tournament.

There is a bracket for each game, and the brackets should be even in numbers. It is not necessary that there be a team for each line, but the number of lines should equal a perfect power of two, such as 4, 8, 16, 32, 64, and 128. If the numbers of teams does not equal one of these figures, the "bye rule" is used. This means that the number of teams should be subtracted from the next highest perfect pow-

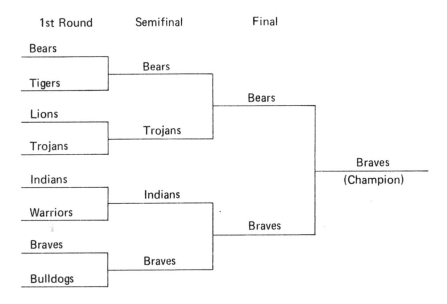

**Figure 6.** Single-Elimination Tournament for Eight Teams

er of two. For example, if there are six teams in a single elimination tournament, six would be subtracted from the next highest power of two. This means that there would be two byes. It is necessary to complete all byes in the first round of a tournament. Figure 7 shows an example illustrating this point.

If the director has some idea of the ability of the participants, he may "seed" them in the tournament. This procedure places the best participants at the opposite ends of the draw, where they will not meet until the semifinals or finals. It may not be fair to seed teams or individuals if points are giv-

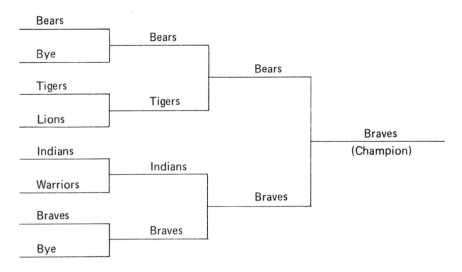

**Figure 7.** Single-Elimination Tournament for Six Teams

en for all-year trophies because it automatically removes the chance of the better teams or players from meeting, while the weaker teams must always play the stronger teams. Third and fourth places can easily be determined by having the semifinalists play.

In most programs, the league play is followed by one of the types of elimination tournaments. A director can easily schedule his fields or courts in advance, even though he does not know which teams will be playing. He schedules the "draw" or game rather than the teams. In this way, he does not have to wait until the leagues are finished to reserve the necessary space and time.

If there are two leagues approaching the final playoffs, the director can schedule the games as follows:

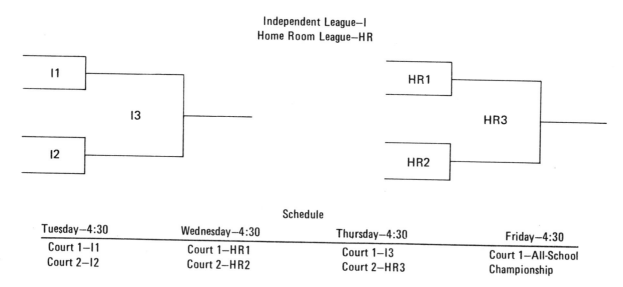

Independent League—I
Home Room League—HR

Schedule

| Tuesday—4:30 | Wednesday—4:30 | Thursday—4:30 | Friday—4:30 |
|---|---|---|---|
| Court 1—I1 | Court 1—HR1 | Court 1—I3 | Court 1—All-School |
| Court 2—I2 | Court 2—HR2 | Court 2—HR3 | Championship |

## CONSOLATION TOURNAMENT

This kind of tournament provides more participation than the single elimination by insuring that each entry plays at least two times. Only the first-round losers go back into the playback or consolation rounds. Figure 8 shows the champion and consolation winner for a draw of eight. Figure 9 shows the same for a draw of seven.

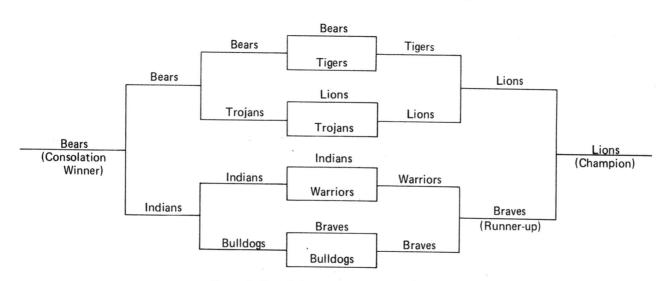

**Figure 8.** Consolation Tournament for Eight Teams

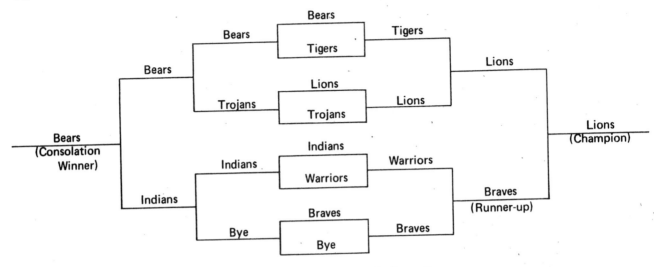

**Figure 9.** Consolation Tournament for Seven Teams

Seeding and byes are treated in the same manner as in single-elimination contests. In the case of byes, the team that loses the first contest played in any round goes into the consolation tournament. If, in Figure 9, the Braves had lost to the Warriors, the Braves would have gone back into the consolation round as it was their first loss.

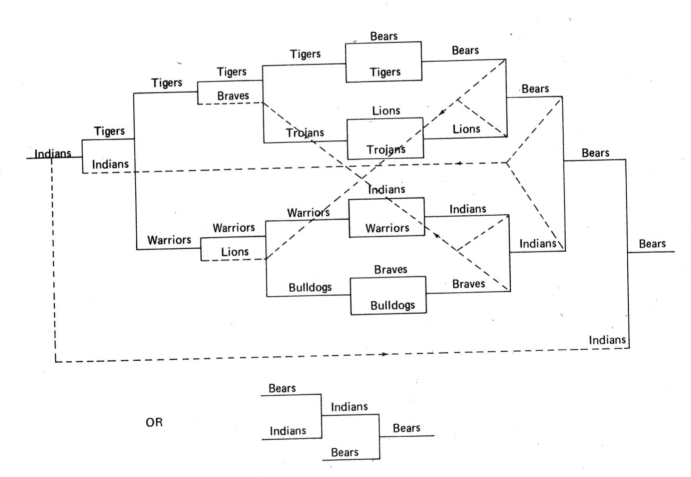

**Figure 10.** Double-Elimination Tournament for Eight Teams

## DOUBLE-ELIMINATION TOURNAMENT

As the name implies, this type of tournament assures that a team will participate until it has lost twice. The draw is similar to the consolation tournament in that the losers go to the left and the winners to the right. Cross bracketing reduces the chances of two teams playing each other more than once. To determine the champion, the winner on the left plays the winner on the right. However, the winner on the left must win two games from the winner on the right because the team on the left has already lost one game. Figure 10 shows an example of this type of tournament.

Another method of conducting a double-elimination tournament is to make a complete new draw among the losers. The teams that have lost twice are dropped, and the teams that have lost once are redrawn with the undefeated teams.

Byes and seeding are handled in the same manner as in the single-elimination tournament. In double-elimination tournaments, there will be one or two less games than twice the number of teams. Consequently, in the example in Figure 10 there will be fourteen or fifteen games, depending upon whether the winner on the right loses one game or none.

A double-elimination tournament, composed of a draw not a perfect power of two, is structurally the same. The byes are merely carried through as you would a losing team from the first round. See Figure 11.

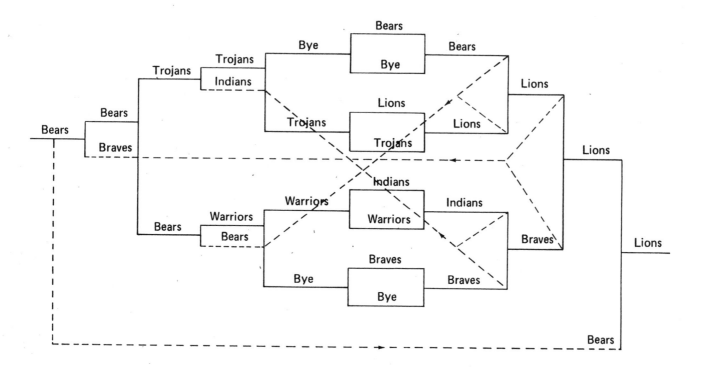

OR

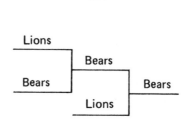

**Figure 11.** Double-Elimination Tournament for Six Teams

## LADDER TOURNAMENT

Ladder tournaments are sometimes an outgrowth of a single or double-elimination competition. In other words, the entries can be placed on a "ladder rung" according to the results of previous tournaments. Figure 12 illustrates a ladder tournament, showing the names of individuals on the rungs of the ladder.

Any appropriate rules may be devised to govern play, but the most widely used plan is to allow a specified time for the competition. A semester, term, or season of the sport may be designated as the length of time the contestants will be permitted to challenge one another. Usually, a player is permitted to challenge only one or two men above him. The loser of a contest should be required to answer a challenge before he is permitted to challenge again. A time limit should be set in which a challenged player must play or forfeit his position on the ladder. Rules of the games and available facilities can be posted with the ladder. Cards, with names, or tags can be placed on small nails or hooks for convenient arrangement .

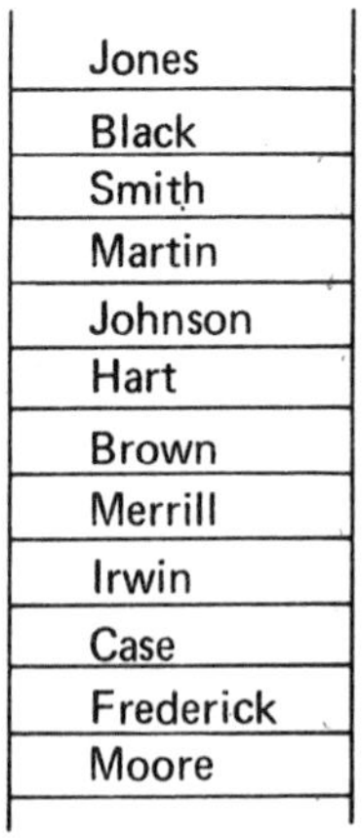

| Jones |
|---|
| Black |
| Smith |
| Martin |
| Johnson |
| Hart |
| Brown |
| Merrill |
| Irwin |
| Case |
| Frederick |
| Moore |

**Figure 12.** Ladder Tournament

## PYRAMID TOURNAMENT

The pyramid is similar to the ladder type of tournament, with the exception that there is more opportunity for challenging. Positions can be given arbitrarily or as the result of other competition. Rules vary from one locality to another, but the challenge rule usually applies in most cases. Generally, a player can challenge anyone in his row. After winning over all opponents in his row, he may challenge anyone in the next row above. Positions are changed as a result of the contests. The pyramid tournament is illustrated in Figure 13.

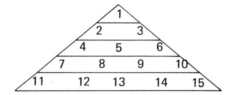

**Figure 13.** Pyramid Tournament

## RINGER TOURNAMENT

This kind of competition can be used primarily for recreative types of activities or other sport skills. The contestant records the best score made each time that he or she plays the course. For example, an individual may have achieved the following score on his first try:

Holes or station: 1 2 3 4 5 6 7 8 9 10
Score: 5 4 4 5 5 3 5 6 4 4

If, on the second time the contestant tried his skill, he scored a four on hole or station four, he would replace the original five and insert his better score of four. Rules are necessary for the purpose of determining the number of times a person may attempt to better himself and for the termination date after which the individual with the best score is declared the winner. Sports skills events and archery require that the contestant enter the highest score at each station, and the subsequent highest total would win.

## TIME-LIMIT TOURNAMENT

This is a special-event type of competition designed to keep large numbers of students involved in various activities at the same time. A number of stations can be set up, both inside and outside the gymnasium. For example, volleyball, a throwing contest, horseshoes, jumping for distance, and free throws might be planned. Each group plays at each area for a certain length of time. At a signal, all action stops and the scores are recorded. The groups and individuals accumulate points from each activity. When all groups have been at each area, the scores are computed and winners recognized. Co-recreative activities are easily adapted to this type of competition.

## FLIGHTS AND QUALIFYING ROUNDS

Qualifying rounds should be used for the purpose of separating the players into various flights for further play. It does not seem justifiable to have qualification requirements for intramural contests if the players who fail to qualify for further competition are eliminated. This procedure limits their participation to one effort.

In qualifying events that have numerical scores, a specified score can be listed as the lowest qualifying score; or a certain number of qualifiers can be designated, such as the highest ten, the second highest ten, and so on.

Another method, illustrated in Figure 14, that can be used for making more equal leagues is a modification of the single-elimination tournament. Considerable time is needed and, therefore, only

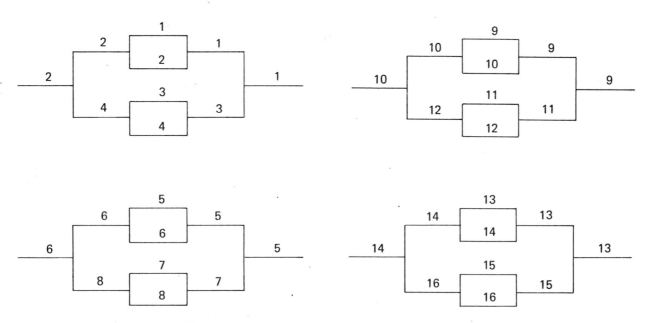

**Figure 14.** Procedure for Placement of Teams in Leagues

a sport conducted during a long season is practical for use with this procedure. The teams may be placed arbitrarily in brackets, and the teams that win two games can be placed in one league (1, 5, 9, 13). The teams that win one and lose one are placed in two other leagues (2, 6, 10, 14) and (3, 7, 11, 15.) The teams that lose two are placed in a fourth league (4, 8, 12, 16). These leagues can then compete for four championships, determined by round-robin play.

### ROUND ROBIN

This type of competition results in a more valid champion because every team has an opportunity to play every other team

One of the first considerations in round-robin play, after the teams have been entered, is to determine the number of games that will be necessary to complete all of the leagues, plus the play-offs. The formula $N \frac{(N-1)}{2}$ will give the number of games in a round robin. N refers to the number of teams entered. For example, if six teams were entered, there would be a total of 15 games. This is computed by substituting in the formula as follows:

$$6 \frac{(6-1)}{2} = 6 \frac{(5)}{2} = \frac{(30)}{2} = 15.$$

Although any number of teams may compete on a round-robin basis, experience has shown that six teams is perhaps the most practical number. This means that each team will play five games, usually one game per week. The school seasons are well adapted to five weeks of play, plus play-off games, to determine league champions and all-school champions. The total group of teams then should be divided into groups or blocks of six—or nearly six—teams. If twenty-four teams were entered in touch football, basketball, or softball, there would be four blocks of six teams each. Each block would require fifteen games to complete the block, making sixty games for the regular schedule. If two blocks of twelve were used, it would take 132 games to complete the regular schedule. This number of games would require many weeks of play. If three blocks of eight were used, there would be three block winners, which might make it difficult to arrange the play-offs fairly. With four blocks of six, the four winning teams could easily be drawn for a four-team, single-elimination tournament.

In drawing up the round-robin schedule, the director may find it convenient to use the following system:

| 1st round | 2nd round | 3rd round | 4th round | 5th round |
|-----------|-----------|-----------|-----------|-----------|
| 1-6       | 1-5       | 1-4       | 1-3       | 1-2       |
| 2-5       | 6-4       | 5-3       | 4-2       | 3-6       |
| 3-4       | 2-3       | 6-2       | 5-6       | 4-5       |

Team names should be substituted for the numbers. It should be noted that the number 1 remains stationary, while the rest of the numbers move in a counter-clockwise fashion. Either direction can be used, as long as the number 1 remains as a fixed number. If there are an unequal number of teams, such as five, the numbers rotate around "X." The "X" in this case does not mean that the team has less games to play; it signifies, rather, that the team has an open date.

| 1st round | 2nd round | 3rd round | 4th round | 5th round |
|-----------|-----------|-----------|-----------|-----------|
| X-5       | X-4       | X-4       | X-2       | X-1       |
| 1-4       | 5-3       | 4-2       | 3-1       | 2-5       |
| 2-3       | 1-2       | 5-1       | 4-5       | 3-4       |

If there are facilities available for three games daily, a six team league or block can be completed in the same number of weeks as a five-team block. Three games a day in a vigorous sport should not be scheduled with five teams because one team would have to play twice in one day.

Using the numbers 1, 2, 3, 4, 5, 6 for each of the teams, it is an easy matter to mimeograph a schedule for each team's games. The days and times can be listed first and the games filled in as indicated in the following example, showing a first-round schedule:

Monday October 20
4:30 P.M.

Field 1. 9A Homeroom (1) vs. 9B Homeroom (6)
Field 2. 9C Homeroom (2) vs. 9D Homeroom (5)
Field 3. 9E Homeroom (3) vs. 9F Homeroom (4)

It may not always be possible, because of certain unavoidable circumstances, to play the needed games each day to complete each series. Postponements are possible because it matters little which games are played first.

The block system is a convenient form for scoring purposes because each block can be numbered with a win and loss column adjacent to the team's name. An easily understood record is then available to the intramural managers and any student who wishes to check the standings.

The standings in round-robin play are often determined on a percentage basis. This is computed by dividing the number of games won by the number of games played. For example, if a team won six games and lost four out of a total of ten games played, ten would be divided into six, giving a percentage of .600.

Another way of determining the standings in round-robin play is to award two points for a victory, one point for a tie, and no points for a defeat. This method differs from the percentage method in that it gives credit for games that end in a tie.

## SOME IMPORTANT AIDS IN SCHEDULE MAKING

The following suggestions are submitted for the purpose of helping the director quickly determine certain necessary information he will need in schedule preparation. N refers to the number of entries.

1. The formula N—1 will determine the number of games necessary to complete a single-elimination tournament.
2. The formula N (2)—1 or 2 will determine the number of games necessary to complete a double-elimination tournament.
3. The formula $\frac{N (N-1)}{2}$ will determine the number of games necessary to complete a round robin.

## Questions for discussion

1. What are some factors which influence the type of organization for competition for intramurals?
2. What are some of the factors which must be taken into consideration when making up an intramural schedule?
3. Under what circumstances may the round robin, double-elimination tournament, single-elimination tournament, and ladder or pyramid-type tournament be used to best advantage?
4. Under what circumstances may the round robin and elimination type of tournament be combined in deciding a champion?
5. How do you determine the number of games to be played in a round robin, double-elimination tournament, and single-elimination tournament?
6. How do you determine the number of byes in an elimination tournament?
7. How do you determine a champion on a percentage basis?
8. What advantage does the procedure of allowing two points for a victory and one point for a tie have over determining a champion on a percentage basis?
9. What are some of the problems encountered in sports that involve meet organization such as track meets, swimming meets, and gymnastic meets?

## Assignments

1. You have the following teams entered for intramural touch football competition: Lions, Tigers, Bears, Wildcats, Bearcats, Panthers, Trojans, and Indians. There are two fields available after school daily (five days per week). You have twenty-nine days in the fall season in which to complete this activity. Draw up a schedule and declare a champion, taking into consideration all of the factors that will influence the type of organization you plan to use. Be sure that you utilize the optimum amount of playing time.

2. You have twelve players signed up for an individual sport. Available for this competition are four game areas on which two games a day may be played. You have the area three days a week for three weeks. Draw up the competition to insure the greatest amount of participation in the time allotted.

## References

*Books*

Lockhart, Aileene, and Mott, Jane A. *Teams and Tournaments*. Fond du Lac, Wisconsin: National Sports Equipment Company, 1954.

Means, Louis E. *Intramurals: Their Organization and Administration*. Englewood Cliffs, New Jersey: Prentice-Hall, Inc., 1963.

Mueller, Pat, and Mitchell, Elmer D. *Intramural Sports*. New York: The Ronald Press, 1960.

*Periodicals*

Halliburton, Jack. "Individual Doubles Tournament Plan." *Scholastic Coach*, vol. 17, September 1947.

Matthews, David. "Basic Fundamentals in Organizing an Intramural Tournament." *The Physiscal Educator*, October 1964.

Mitchell, Viola. "A Method of Arranging and Recording a Round Robin Tournament for Any Number of Teams or Individuals." *Journal of Health and Physical Education*, vol. 18, June 1947.

Swegan, Don. "A Ladder Tournament for Individual Sports." *Scholastic Coach*, October 1955.

# Financing
# The Intramural Program

## BASIC CONSIDERATIONS

Intramural programs receive their financial support in various ways. Because this program is usually developed after many of the other activities have become established, it is often put on a self-supporting basis. If an energetic and resourceful director can raise the necessary funds, the program is conducted on a relatively satisfactory basis. If funds are not available, the students are deprived of the opportunity to participate. If limited funds are available, all students should receive some recreational benefits—rather than services for boys and men only, and very limited or no services for girls and women. All students are deserving of whatever intramural services can be provided with the available funds.

The director of intramurals must assume responsibility for obtaining necessary finances to provide services that will be utilized by intramural participants. The director's ability to interpret the services; the need for adequate funding; and the participants' involvement will directly affect financing and, therefore, the program. Communication regarding the intramural program and the concept of services is the immediate responsibility of the director. Communication and rapport with students, faculty, and community will be necessary to obtain financial support and reflect accountability for the investment made.

An attempt has been made throughout this text to point out that the provision of a comprehensive, intelligently conducted intramural program adds to the value of education at any level. Since participation in properly organized intramural activities is an important part of the educational process, provision should be made for it in the school budget. On the high-school level, the board of education should appropriate funds for this purpose. In the colleges and universities, the governing board should designate funds, either directly to student services for the intramural program, or include the necessary funds in the total athletic or physical education budget. A problem arises in some states where public funds may not be used for the purchase of awards. This item should be of minor concern, however, as evidenced by the discussion of awards in Unit XII.

## ADVANTAGES AND DISADVANTAGES OF VARIOUS PLANS

The intramural program should not have to depend upon the gate receipts of the athletic teams for its funds. As a matter of fact, the varsity teams should not be expected to rely on this method of financing the interscholastic athletic program. Both programs should be supported as valid parts of the total educational opportunities offered. Because of the close affiliation with the athletic department, school administrators very often place the funds for intramurals under the director of athletics. As long as the money is clearly allotted for intramural use only, it matters little whether the responsible person is the principal, athletic director, or others. Too many times, however, there is no clearly defined allotment, and the intramural funds become depleted in favor of other needs.

Under less favorable conditions, school administrators may designate a certain percentage of the varsity gate receipts to intramurals. This type of financial budget predetermines the success or failure of many high school intramural programs from year to year, and even from season to season. The director may find it extremely difficult to plan for the future because he may not be sure of the finances available. Money from gate receipts may come grudgingly because the receipts are oftentimes inadequate. If the school system follows a plan of self-support for interscholastic athletics, the athletic director may not be too happy to place additional strain on his limited budget. If this is the only possible source of funds, then the intramural director must make the best of it. It should be understood, however, that a newly appointed intramural director may not be in a position to determine the source of his funds. By creating an adequate program and justifying the cost, he should be able to secure a more stable budget.

Close cooperation with the athletic coaches and physical education teachers is obviously of paramount importance. The scope of intramural services can be increased through cooperation in the use or development of physical facilities; joint use of equipment and mutual interest in program and services can economize on time and budget expenditure. Intramural services require purchasing equipment and awards and obtaining labor for supervision or officiating. Whenever cooperative use of equipment is possible, an immediate saving is made and other activity investments are made possible. Duplication of services, equipment, and program is not necessary when the same clientele is being served. The total physical-activity program will be expanded for all students with effective administration of investment.

Special care should be taken to avoid the use of old, faulty equipment in an attempt to economize. The participants' safety is most important, and good equipment is necessary to permit good game play. Safety hazards become much more evident when second-hand equipment is used. The equipment probably has already been well used and is in need of close inspection to insure safe play. Examples of second-hand equipment to be most careful of includes: old catcher's masks, protectors, mats, standards for nets, and gymnastic equipment. Homemade equipment must be confined to use in those activities in which the safety of the participants is not dependent upon the equipment.

There are specific areas in which savings can be made through the effective use of volunteer service. Interested students can assist in lining fields; laying out improvised fields or play areas; improving room space for a fitness or game center; helping to officiate, score, time, guard at the pool; or supervising other specific activities.

Promoting intramural services on a regular basis may be determined by the school administration—and the necessary fiscal responsibility assumed with a specific budget allotted by the board of education. The administration could offer assistance in funding the intramural services through contingency funds for special projects. However, a student body should always be encouraged to contribute to better services and a better program and creatively assist in improving opportunities. Funds raised may be effectively used for purchase of new equipment, awards, developing new fitness areas or weight rooms, or to cover operating expenses if necessary. Intramural sports for all students naturally calls for the participation and the involvement of all and an open opportunity for contributing ideas and methods to improve services and program offerings.

Charging admission for certain intramural events is one of the most widely used methods of obtaining funds other than from *specific* budgets or gate receipts. Some of the *most common* events are exhibitions, sport nights, water shows, fitness demonstrations, splash parties, dance concerts, and special dances (rock, fifties' style, square, or Greek and Israeli line). With advance publicity, and the reason for the activity clearly announced, a good attendance is generally assured. Open activities available to all students are most appropriate and successful; however, much interest can be generated in participating in special events planned to serve specific, smaller groups in popular physical activities. Combinations of the following people could result in improved communications and services, with less mass participation and crowding of the facilities: father-sons, father-daughters, mother-daughters, mother-sons, total families, freshmen, sophomores, juniors, seniors, alums, mixed classes, clubs, faculty-students, and faculty parents. One of the greatest disadvantages of planning activities to raise revenue is the tremendous amount of time taken to organize such a program or event—time that could be invested in conducting a better activity program for students. Plans that include the intramural activities themselves are likely to help the program more, in the long run, than strictly money-making schemes.

Other plans which have been used successfully in many schools include:

1. Candy sales
2. Plays
3. Bake sales
4. Rummage sales
5. Scrap paper and junk drives
6. Donations
7. Admission charge for movies
8. Percentage of food concessions a varsity games
9. School activity fee at the beginning of the year to include all extra-class events

## Questions for discussion

1. What do you consider the best plan for financing the intramural program on the secondary school level? The college level? Support your answer.
2. What are some of the advantages and disadvantages of financing the intramural program from the athletic association budget?
3. Under what circumstances is it justifiable to charge an entrance fee for intramural participation?
4. What are some of the advantages and disadvantages of the various methods of raising funds for the intramural program?

## Assignments

1. Set up a budget for one semester for a program consisting of touch football, basketball, free throwing, horseshoes, and a special event such as a field day.

2. Survey the various methods of obtaining funds for the intramural sports program. Write a summary indicating the advantages and disadvantages of each.

## References

*Books*

Hughes, William L., and Williams, Jesse F. *Sports: Their Organization and Administration.* New York: A. S. Barnes & Company, 1944, pp. 178-180.

Means, Louis E. *Intramurals: Their Organization and Administration.* Englewood Cliffs, New Jersey: Prentice-Hall, Inc., 1963.

Scott, Harry. *Competitive Sports in Schools and Colleges,* chapter XI. New York: Harper and Brothers, 1951.

Voltmer, Carl D. and Lapp, Vernon W. *The Intramural Handbook,* chapter II. St. Louis: The C.V. Mosby Company.

*Periodicals*

Cherry, H. S. "Survey Report on Financing College Intramurals." *College Physical Education Association Proceedings,* 1953.

DeNike, Howard R. "How Good is Your Intramural Sports Program?" *The Physical Educator*, October 1965.

Kraus, Richard. "Which Way School Recreation?" *Journal of Health, Physical Education and Recreation*, November-December 1965.

# Promotion of the Intramural Program

## SOME FACTORS TO CONSIDER IN PROGRAM PROMOTION

The promotion of any intramural program can best be accomplished by the quality of the program itself. As mentioned previously, the participation in a well-organized program offers much to the total education of the student. Therefore, any means by which the shy or backward student can be induced to participate appears justifiable. The number of methods used to publicize and promote an intramural program may be of little value if the activities offered are few in number and haphazardly conducted. Promotion of the program may be arbitrarily divided into the following three phases: (1) the program and its administration; (2) notification of potential participants; and (3) stimulation of public support through desirable public relations. Obviously, a great deal of overlapping exists between all three of these phases, but they are distinct enough to be discussed separately.

## ADMINISTRATION OF THE PROGRAM

The person responsible for the program must be interested in the program and the participants. This individual must be willing to take time to make modifications of schedules and be tolerant of conflicts of time that are certain to arise. However, participation and game play should be regarded more important than efficient scheduling and administration.

Emphasis on equal participation for all should be stressed. In this connection, it is important to remember that equality may be brought about by instruction in skills. In many high schools, the intramural director is also directly concerned with the physical education classes and, therefore, is in a position to improve the skills of the students. Point-and-award systems should be carefully planned so that all have equal opportunity to score or receive some form of recognition.

The spirit of intramural activity is participation, and rules and technicalities which tend to reduce participation might well be eliminated. The director should be interested in the number of participants as well as the quality of performance. Students are quick to recognize the degree of sincerity displayed by the director toward them and the program. In the final analysis, the personal interest of the director is likely to be a determining factor in the promotion of the program.

## NOTIFICATION OF POTENTIAL PARTICIPANTS

This is a very important phase in the promotion of intramural activities. However, its implementation gives rise to numerous problems. In general, students are not likely to read notices and bulletins comprehensively—and since the printed word is one of the most common means of publicizing the program, it becomes clear that many students may miss the information intended for them. The following list indicates some of the ways in which information in printed form may be distributed:

1. Mimeographed circulars
2. Bulletins to homerooms and organizations       .
3. Posters
4. Bulletin boards
5. Community newspapers
6. School paper
7. Intramural department news sheet

Certain basic procedures are required for use of the above methods. The information should be posted or distributed early enough for individuals and teams to organize and practice for the event. Use of color figures or large letters is important to attract attention. The information must be presented in understandable terms so that the type of event, place, and time are quickly noticed.

Most schools have mimeographing machines available. Stencils of any design may be cut with little experience. In some cases, this procedure has been used as a part of a project of the commerical department.

Mineographed material, posted on all bulletin boards and read in homerooms and other classes, is an efficient method of publicizing the program. It is important to keep the information on bulletin boards up-to-date and neatly arranged. If the students frequently find old information on a board they may soon cease to look at the board at all. It must be remembered that people who are going to read the material on a bulletin board are usually on their way to another location. They will perhaps stop to read only if the arrangement is appealing and the information is direct and interesting. Tournament draws and league schedules can be displayed to good advantage on intramural bulletin boards. Brief instructions regarding methods of play and deadlines should accompany the draw sheets.

Instant printing methods are now available and popular in schools. New materials and printing methods, such as silk screen and offset print, provide attractive materials. Designs and written material can be tastefully produced in a variety of colors by students or staff. Current interest in journalism, art and design, copying, and printing vocations has increased the availability of reproduction equipment as well as staff for teaching and consultation. Student awareness of the various departments, equipment, and materials permits a more integrated educational experience for the student. Utilization of all school services permits a better sense of community and endeavor for all participants.

Other methods of disseminating intramural information include the following:

1. Assemblies
2. Sports meetings
3. Homeroom and class announcements
4. School public-address system or radio
5. Orientation programs
6. Loop films regarding program

The use of these devices is basically the same as the written methods. Announcements must be timely, clear, and concise. A very successful method of creating interest, channeling information, and insuring participation is to call meetings for the activity that is about to start. Students who have signed up to play, as well as those who have not, should be urged to attend the meeting. At this time, rules, techniques, use of facilities, and playing times can be discussed.

At the college level, the orientation program at the beginning of the school year can be profitable for incoming freshmen. Information about facilities and activities available for students can do much to make the new and younger students feel at home in new surroundings. Information centers and a telephone information service can be combined to give all students daily information regarding intramural services. Employed or volunteer students can assume meaningful roles in interpreting and giving pertinent information to orient students to the total intramural program.

The total intramural program can be promoted through effective communication only when goals and objectives are totally integrated for men and women. Small differences in program can exist, but the overall, complete program should be the same for all students. The services can only be interpreted and promoted when the same program exists fundamentally for all students. Care and attention must be given to assure similar hours, activities, and eligibility. Communication is difficult on large and small campuses; and clearly defining one program "for all" promotes participation by all and stability in utilizing facilities. Also, women students can benefit from the men having had more emphasis placed on traditional intramural sport. Men students can readily interpret programs, eligibility rules, awards, points, and game play. Incorporating men into the communication structure can encourage women to participate in intramural activity and may increase participation by more than half. Complete separation of sexes in sport has not permitted separate-but-equal opportunities in sport.

## ENCOURAGING PUBLIC SUPPORT

The intramural program that provides for wholesome and interesting activities for all students should be well accepted by the community. The following list enumerates various methods that have been used successfully in obtaining public interest in intramurals:

1. Open house
2. Sports nights
3. Parents' nights
4. Community newspaper coverage
5. Parent-Teachers Association meetings
6. Radio and television presentations
7. Service club talks
8. Intramural handbooks
9. Championship games open to the public
10. Notices to parents through students
11. Photographs of sport action and participants
12. Action films of program participation

The material distributed by the above methods should be of an informational type. If the average adult is exposed to the information concerning a good intramural program, his support is more likely to be obtained. Adults, in general, do not react favorably to high pressure tactics from the schools. If it can be shown that students benefit by the program, public support will usually be forthcoming. Community support does not necessarily mean financial aid. Permission for corecreational activities, after-dinner programs, use of civic facilities, and increased school facilities are evidences of community approval.

A report should be compiled each semester or year, as seems necessary. This report should include the number and variety of activities offered and the number of students participating in each event. It is not imperative that the exact number of different students participating be listed. This would, perhaps, take an unjustifiable amount of time. This report is important in showing the interest of the students and the need for facilities and equipment. It might well be submitted for publication in the local community newspapers.

An intramural handbook can serve a useful purpose in promoting the program. Handbooks can be mimeographed, with color sheets for covers. These handbooks can be issued free or at a nominal fee to the students and at events that include parents and other adults.

A variety of the methods discussed here can be used to ensure that program information reaches as many students and adults as possible. A very important consideration is the guarantee that each student hears or reads about the activities offered. In a well-organized program, the participating students will promote the program by word of mouth. This is one of the best ways to increase the size and value of the intramural program.

## Questions for discussion

1. How may bulletin boards be used to promote an intramural program?
2. To what extent may bulletins be used on the secondary school level? The college level?
3. What are some of the problems involved in developing an intramural handbook?
4. What are the possibilities of promoting the intramural program through regular physical education classes, homerooms, school papers, and assemblies?
5. What do you consider the best medium for promoting the intramural program on the secondary school level? On the college level? Support your answer.
6. What are some ways of gaining community support for the intramural program?
7. What part do field days play in promoting the intramural program?

## Assignment

1. Plan a special event such as an open house, sports night, or field day. Include all factors which are involved in setting up an event.

## References

*Books*

Means, Louis E. *Intramurals: Their Organization and Administration.* Englewood Cliffs, New Jersey: Prentice-Hall, Inc., 1963.

*Periodicals*

Boycheff, Kooman. "Promotion of Intramural Sports through Photography." *College Physical Education Association Proceedings,* 1962.

Beeman, H. F. "Intramural Publicity Through Television, Radio, and Visual Aids." *College Physical Education Association Proceedings,* 1959.

Buchanan, Edsel. "Interpreting Intramurals to the Faculty." *The Physical Educator,* May 1966.

Bucher, Charles A. "Field Days." *Journal of Health and Physical Education* vol. 19, January 1948.

Cherry, H. S. "Motivation and Promotion of an Intramural Program." *College Physical Education Association Proceedings,* 1955.

Dodson, Taylor. "Public Relations for the Intramural Program." *The Physical Educator vol. IX,* March 1952.

Higgins, Joseph. "Intramural Sports and New Dimensions in Residential Education." *National Intramural Association Proceedings,* 1966.

Leibrock, Phillip J. "Intramural Publicity and Public Relations." *The Physical Educator,* October 1965.

Newton, Donald M. "Public Relations-Publicity-Promotion in Intramurals." *National Intramural Association Proceedings,* 1966.

Unruh, Dan W. "Awards, New Ideals, and Promotional Techniques." *National Intramural Associaton Proceedings,* 1966.

# Corecreation and Club Activities

## IMPORTANCE OF CORECREATION

Increasing emphasis has been placed on integrated activity for boys and girls and men and women. Coed intramurals, club sports, and physical education classes have become popular in schools and colleges. A conscientious director will realize the important place of corecreational activities and will plan areas of the program to serve this interest. All students appreciate the opportunity to engage in recreative activity under varying circumstances and varying participant arrangements. Integrated activity for men and women presents a very realistic and useful activity experience which promotes the lifetime sport orientation of individuals and, therefore, families. Successful competition and recreation encourage all of the participants to have a non-sexist view of sport and game and encourage everyone to participate and be involved. Sport and game have a tradition of separateness for boys and girls and men and women. There is always opportunity for separate competition; but integrated activity is important, rather new, and gaining participation and emphasis in high schools and colleges.

The development of sports clubs is one of the most dynamic changes on the college and university level. Many universities now help and support many different clubs. These groups may vary from a Chinese boxing club with 10 members to a ski club with 1,500 members. The martial arts and outdoor sports (skiing, sailing, cycling, and hiking) seem to be receiving much attention currently.

The sport culture of the high school and college may find the greatest growth and development in this area of club sport. The majority of people wishing to have an activity experience are served well and democratically in this area. Here, men and women create for themselves an opportunity to concentrate on a particular sport or activity and progress in skill and participation at their own speed. Beginners, intermediate, and advanced students are motivated to learn and proceed while teaching and learning. Because of the mixed levels of proficiency within the club, a natural motivation and learning situation exists. Care and attention for learning are shared among club members, with the progress receiving very personalized and continuing attention. Participants' success is recognized and actually celebrated by other members because of the reciprocal teaching and learning investment of the people.

Club sport attracts not only students, but faculty, staff, and community members. A very open atmosphere, with open membership, allows the sport or activity to belong to the people involved. Special consideration and attention of the intramural director should insure the openness and availability of the club and promote and encourage creative, new means of supporting club endeavors. Directors should be prepared to assist in the formation and development of new clubs. Aid may be received in the form of meeting rooms, gymnasiums, club rooms, fields, mimeograph facilities, or liaison with other campus departments. However, the club should be student-motivated and controlled.

All clubs must meet requirements, such as those associated with safety, equal opportunities for all students, and other local regulations. Another basic requirement should be the development of a training program to teach students the skills around which the club is formed.

## DIFFERENCE IN PERSPECTIVE

The way in which corecreational activities are conducted determines largely the enthusiasm and success that the activities will enjoy. The director must remember that in this part of the program there should be a great deal of interest in equal enjoyable participation rather than an intensely competitive atmosphere.

In planning corecreational activities, it may be advisable to arrange a combination of opportunities for single days or nights or events—or a regularly scheduled league, with play at least once or twice a week for approximately four or five weeks. Emphasis should always remain on participating in sport and activity for enjoyment and relaxation, with attention placed on the camaraderie among the members and opposing team members. The social experience should be at least equal to the game experience in importance. A harsh, competitive atmosphere would not permit open game play and equal participation for both men and women.

The noon hour makes an excellent time for corecreational activities on an informal basis. Mixers, sports nights, and open houses are used by some schools to provide corecreational activities for students. Also, these kinds of events provide a fine means of introducing mixed activity to the community. Proper orientation is important in many communities before mixed activities will be fully accepted. The open house event, in which the adults can join in and see for themselves the fun and obvious values, is an excellent means of orientation.

## POSSIBLE ACTIVITIES

In general, activities engaged in by both sexes should not be of a highly competitive nature or in which unnecessary injury could be sustained by the participant. Activities should be selected according to strength and endurance differences. It is suggested that games and contests requiring body contact not be included. However, specific games and contests resulting in collision of bodies must be evaluated on the values of the sport as a corecreational sport and modified to insure safe play. Some attempt may be made in classifying teams according to body type and skill to encourage a positive game experience. Currently, much discussion and interest exist in permitting play among people who wish to participate together in sport. A responsibility does exist for intramural administrators to assist and provide these people with safe and enjoyable playing conditions. League play, informal pick-up games, short or long-range individual tournaments, special evenings, and sports clubs—all should contribute to providing a means by which all people can have their special interest served.

Suggested activities that are popular areas of corecreational participation:

1. Archery
2. Badminton
3. Billiards
4. Bowling
5. Canoeing and kayak
6. Card and table games
7. Cross country (skiing and running)
8. Cycling
9. Dancing
10. Fencing
11. Flying and soaring
12. Golf
13. Hiking
14. Horseshoes
15. Jogging
16. Judo
17. Karate
18. Riding
19. Riflery
20. Sailing
21. Scuba diving
22. Shuffleboard
23. Skiing
24. Slow-pitch softball
25. Swimming (speed, distance, synchronized, diving)
26. Table tennis
27. Tennis
28. Track and field
29. Volleyball
30. Yoga

## ORGANIZATIONAL ASSISTANCE

In most schools, there are clubs sponsored to meet the individual interests of students. Some of these include language club, dramatic club, journalism club, ecology club, and other subject matter groups.

Some clubs are made up of mixed groups, while others segregate boys and girls. Aside from their particular interest, all of these organizations are concerned with the students and their development. By encouraging these clubs to take part, and also to sponsor some of the corecreational activities, a great amount of social value can be achieved. Rather than remaining separate entities by themselves, the students have an opportunity to see how all of the other groups contribute to the student's total educational experience. Clubs and groups that are integrated may form a natural catalyst for beginning and promoting corecreational sport activity.

## SEASONAL ACTIVITIES

Depending upon the locality and climate, many outdoor activities based on weather make for fine corecreational gatherings. Sledding, toboganning, and skating in the winter; swimming and splash parties in late spring; and hiking in all seasons are a few outstanding examples.

There appears to be little opposition at the present time to supervised mixed activity of the above pastimes. A major problem is how to provide these wholesome experiences for the students. With imagination and intelligent use of all available facilities, coupled with complete cooperation of the boys' and girls' physical education departments, a satisfactory corecreational program can take place on an intramural basis.

### Questions for discussion

1. What should the philosophy of intramural directors be with regard to corecreational activities?
2. What values can be realized by students who participate in corecreational programs?
3. In what different way should the participation in games be stressed when the sexes are mixed?
4. What types of relationships may clubs and organizations have with the intramural program?
5. How could the ecology club and the journalism club of a school contribute to the intramural program?

### Assignments

1. Describe the administrative problems which would have to be considered in organizing and conducting a gym night and splash party for boys and girls in a senior high school.
2. Organize an all-school outing of any kind. Show how you would use the various clubs and organizations of the school, in cooperation with the intramural department, in planning and conducting the outing.
3. Discuss the arrangement necessary to prepare for a mixed track and field or swimming meet.
4. Discuss rule modifications that may be necessary in a particular corecreational sport.
5. Consider club sport and its role in serving individual student skill needs.

### References

*Books*

Kleindienst, Viola, and Weston, Arthur. *Intramural and Recreation Programs for Schools and Colleges.* New York: Appleton-Century-Crofts, 1964.

Means, Louis Edgar. *Intramurals: Their Organization and Administration.* Englewood Cliffs, New Jersey: Prentice-Hall, Inc., 1963.

Mueller, Pat, and Mitchell, Elmer D. *Intramural Sports*. New York: The Ronald Press Company, 1964.


*Periodicals*

Buchanan, Edsel. "Co-Recreation." *National Intramural Association Proceedings,* 1961.

Copeland, Dodd. "Intramural Through Sports Clubs." *Scholastic Coach* vol. 18, October 1948.

England, Earle W. "The Adaption of Activities to a Coeducational Intramural Program." *The Physical Educator,* May 1968.

Gehrke, Delbert, and Slebos, Warren. "Guys and Gals Intramurals." *Journal of Health, Physical Education and Recreation,* 1972.

Haniford, G. W. "Problems in Co-recreational Sports." *College Physical Education Association Proceedings,* 1956.

MacIntyre, Christine M. "Co-Recreation—A Must For the Future." *National Intramural Association Proceedings,* 1966.

Matthews, David. "Sports Club Organization." *Scholastic Coach,* January 1965.

Sliger, Ira T. "Extensive Sports Club Program." *Journal of Health, Physical Education and Recreation,* February 1970.

# Extramurals

## THE MEANING OF EXTRAMURALS

The term "extramurals" is used to describe those intramural activities which are conducted beyond the immediate surroundings of the school. These activities are carried on between the intramural teams and players of different schools. As a rule there are few, if any, eligibility requirements and gate receipt problems similar to those connected with interscholastic athletic programs. Usually the contests are arranged between schools at various times, with no attempt made to complete a regular schedule as is the case in the varsity sports.

In the broadcast sense, extramurals could cover any activities or sports conducted between two or more schools. However, there are clear differences in location, organization, scheduling and perspective between an extramural program, intercollegiate or club sports and, of course, intramurals. It was shown earlier that intramural activities were held within the confines of a school or college, between groups or teams from that institution.

Interscholastic and intercollegiate programs encompass much more organization involving coaches, tryouts and practices. In addition, long range scheduling over a number of years is required for successful competition on a league basis. Varsity programs exist to win championships. Extramural programs should stress wider participation regardless of the skill of the players.

## ADVANTAGES AND DISADVANTAGES

One of the values of an extramural program lies in the fact that students who are not on varsity teams have the opportunity to visit other schools and compete with students other than their own schoolmates. It will be shown later how this may be accomplished with a planned program of activities with other schools. The disadvantage of these interschool contests in some cases outweigh the advantages. The greatest danger may be to the intramural program itself. It is possible that intramural teams might be neglected in an effort to produce a better team that could win in the extramural contests.

Some intramural directors feel that the time spent on practice, scheduling, and preparation for an extramural contest might be much better devoted to enlargement or improvement of the intramural program.

## ACCEPTABLE PRACTICES

There are methods by which the values of extramural activities can be realized without encountering certain disadvantages attributed to this type of program. One way is by the establishment of play days or sports days. Both of these types of activity can involve a large number of students and faculty members. Many different games and contests can be scheduled throughout the day, and a picnic-type lunch can be served by the host school. The play day permits students from various schools to meet each other in friendly competition on teams composed of players from each school. The sports day is organized so that the teams represent their own schools without the exchange of players. It seems advisable to have the play day and sports day open to all students rather than to only the best intramural teams in the school. This plan has been used by many girls' athletic associations as a means of providing competition without the problems that beset the boys' varsity teams. The intramural director, as well as the rest of the faculty, should be included in the planning and administration of the activities. It can then become an entire school project, which may appear more justifiable than an interscholastic schedule of intramural teams.

Another way of securing extra-school activity, without the intramural director becoming involved as a coach, is the challenge method. One of the main features in the extramural athletic games is the source of the interest and the promotional energy. The director need not always provide the impetus for participation in extramural games. A group of students may desire to meet another group of students from another school in any type of contest. For example, in colleges and universities, it may be a fraternity, sorority or a residence hall team that issues a challenge to its counterpart at a neighboring school. This type of interest is desirable, and it might well be supported further by the director. He might attempt to aid the groups by allowing them the use of the facilities, equipment, and officials usually provided for intramural teams. Many colleges and some high schools follow this practice at the present time. The games are sometimes scheduled in conjunction with the varsity game between the schools in a particular sport. The challenge game is usually played before the varsity contest, and informal social activities are sometimes arranged for the visiting players. In this way, the director does not need to become involved as an intramural coach. The teams may be the best or worst in the school, with the whole affair being conducted in a spirit of fun and the mutual interest of the participants.

## NEW SPORTS DEVELOPMENT

There is undoubtedly a definite need for recognition of those activities which have not reached varsity status. These activities may be promoted by sports clubs or be conducted by the city recreation program. After an activity has proved popular and has sustained interest for a period of time, petitions by students may result in a varsity team being formed. However, it should be borne in mind that it is not the purpose of the intramural program to enlarge the varsity program by promoting various sports. On the contrary, the time and energy of the director, for the most part, should be devoted to the development of an interesting and comprehensive intramural program for all students in the school. Providing recreative services for all of the people is very important because skilled participants in varsity competition are only a minority of the students being involved and supported in their sports interest.

### Questions for discussion

1. What is meant by the term "extramural"?
2. Under what circumstances are extramurals most practical?
3. What influence will extramurals have on interscholastic athletics?
4. What are some objections to extramurals?
5. What is the difference between "intramurals," "extramurals," and "interscholastics"?

### Assignment

1. Write a summary indicating how you might allow an activity to be played on an extramural basis without becoming involved yourself (as intramural director).

## References

*Books*

Kleindienst, Viola, and Weston, Arthur. *Intramural and Recreation Programs for Schools and Colleges.* New York: Appleton-Century-Crofts, 1964.

Means, Louis Edgar. *Intramurals: Their Organization and Administration.* Englewood Cliffs, New Jersey: Prentice-Hall, 1963.

Scott, Harry. *Competitive Sports in Schools and Colleges,* chapter XI. New York: Harper and Brothers, 1951.

*Periodicals*

Asip, William M. and Campbell, Loren D. "Extramural Sports Day." *The Physical Educator,* May 1958.

Dodson, Taylor. "Developing an Extramural Sports Day." *The Physical Educator,* October 1958.

Mendelsohn, E. J. "Recent Trends and Developments of Extramural Activities in Colleges and Universities." *College Physical Education Association Proceedings,* 1956.

Rice, Robert J. "Extramurals." *Journal of Health, Physical Education and Recreation,* November 1959.

Riordan, William. "Extramural Sports Festivals." *National Intramural Association Proceedings,* 1961.

# Evaluation of the Intramural Program

## PURPOSES OF EVALUATION

Evaluation of the intramural program serves a number of distinct purposes. A satisfactory program evaluation should determine how well the program meets the activity needs of the students as well as determining if there is enough variety of activity. In addition, information may be gathered on such factors as adequacy of contests in the activities offered, competency of officiating and supervision, and availability of equipment. Evaluation may also reveal the extent of leadership opportunities, the degree of cooperation among students, the degree of skills attained, and the influence that the program has on student health attitudes and practices.

## EVALUATING FOR ADMINISTRATIVE WEAKNESSES

One of the most common signs of disinterest in the program is a number of forfeited games and contests. If the games are scheduled at a time of conflicting events and the rules of the sport are modified to the extent that the activity becomes uninteresting, or if the contestants are not well matched, there are likely to be many forfeits. The director must attempt to reduce the factors that encourage the forfeiting of games, and this may be done in preliminary planning.

Numerous forfeits in a particular sport, or at a specific time, should indicate to the director that certain modifications may be necessary. For example, disproportionate scores of games may be an indication of improper classification for competition. This inequity might lead to teams forfeiting contests in order to avoid humiliating defeat. The alert director can remedy this situation by improving the method of classification of students for competition.

Postponements that are arranged with the intramural director in advance usually signify interest in the program. The teams that are interested enough to want to play the game and ask that it be rescheduled, and also make their own arrangements, have a definite interest in the sport. If they did not care about the outcome or have a desire to participate, they would not show up at the scheduled time.

Most postponements are brought about by other school activities that involve most of the student body. The director can, with a calendar of events, schedule the games so that there will be little conflict with most of the other activities. There will, perhaps, be some unavoidable conflicts that no one can foresee. However, it seems advisable that postponements should be granted and the activities rescheduled whenever a justifiable reason is given, because the program is based on participation, and not on the speed with which a tournament is completed.

Protests are usually concerned with two factors. These involve the ability of the official and his interpretation of the rules and the eligibility of an intramural participant. Simple eligibility rules, prominently displayed and discussed, will do much to reduce the ineligible player protest. This type of protest does not tell the director too much about the program except that the rules on eligibility may need clarification or modification.

Many protests on the ability and judgment of officials can cause a great deal of dissatisfaction with the program. If one particular official is constantly involved, the obvious solution is to dismiss him. If there are several protests each week, the entire group of officials should be called to a meeting for the purpose of clarification of rules. The officials must understand that they are to provide a service to the participants. At the same time, it is extremely important that all participants show respect to those persons who officiate the activities. Occasional protests are not evidence of general dissatisfaction; protests of close games may often show the intense interest and desire of the teams to win. These protests are not to be encouraged, but the privilege to protest should be recognized.

## NUMBER OF PARTICIPANTS

The number of teams or individuals who sign up for the various activities can be used as a measuring stick to determine the degree of interest in the program. The director should not be primarily interested in the number of participants. Numbers should come only as a result of open facilities and available equipment and an interesting and properly supervised activity. Conducting certain events in a manner designed primarily to increase numbers of participants may not be sound administration. By keeping records of the number of students participating in each event, the director can tell whether certain modifications and improvements are necessary. Also, important data can be obtained in comparing attendance or participation to cost accounting, accidents and safety, personnel analyses, space utilization, and development.

## OTHER METHODS OF EVALUATION

The questionnaire method is a suitable way to collect a large amount of information in a relatively short time. One of the limitations of this method is concerned with the development of a satisfactory list of questions and at the same time with receiving valid answers to the questions. However, a good questionnaire should serve both as a publicity measure and as a data gathering device. The director can study the results and plan modifications as seem necessary. In this connection, care must be taken because some students may answer the questions in a manner which they think will please the director.

Interviews and suggestion boxes sometimes bring good results because students are likely to speak frankly about something they do not like. Student officials and supervisors can gather information from the intramural teams during the season. The intramural players will generally not hesitate to voice their opinions and desires to these intramural workers. In this regard, caution must be exercised lest the opinion of a dissenting few be accepted as that of the majority.

### Questions for discussion

1. Of what value are questionnaire studies in evaluating an intramural program?
2. What are some of the ways of determining the quality of performance and conduct in an intramural program?
3. What will the number of protests, forfeits, and postponements tell you about the intramural program?
4. How can you determine the growth of a program through statistics? Can this be determined entirely?

## Assignments

1. Devise a check list of criteria for evaluating an intramural program. Weight the criteria for importance.

2. Write a brief summary on what you consider the best way to evaluate an intramural program.

## References

*Books*

Huelte, George, and Shirers, Jay. *Public Administration of Recreation Services.* Philadelphia: Lea and Febiger, 1972.

Voltmer, Edward F., and Esslinger, Arthur A. *The Organization and Administration of Physical Edcation* 3rd edition, chapter 9. New York: Appleton-Century-Crofts, Inc., 1958.

*Periodicals*

Anderson, Don. "Intramural Sports in A Changing Society." *Journal of Health, Physical Education, and Recreation,* November-December 1971.

DeNike, Howard. "How Good Is Your Intramural Sports Program?" *The Physical Educator,* October 1965.

Hyatt, Ronald. "Evaluation In Intramurals." *Journal of Health, Physical Education and Recreation,* June 1971.

Appendix

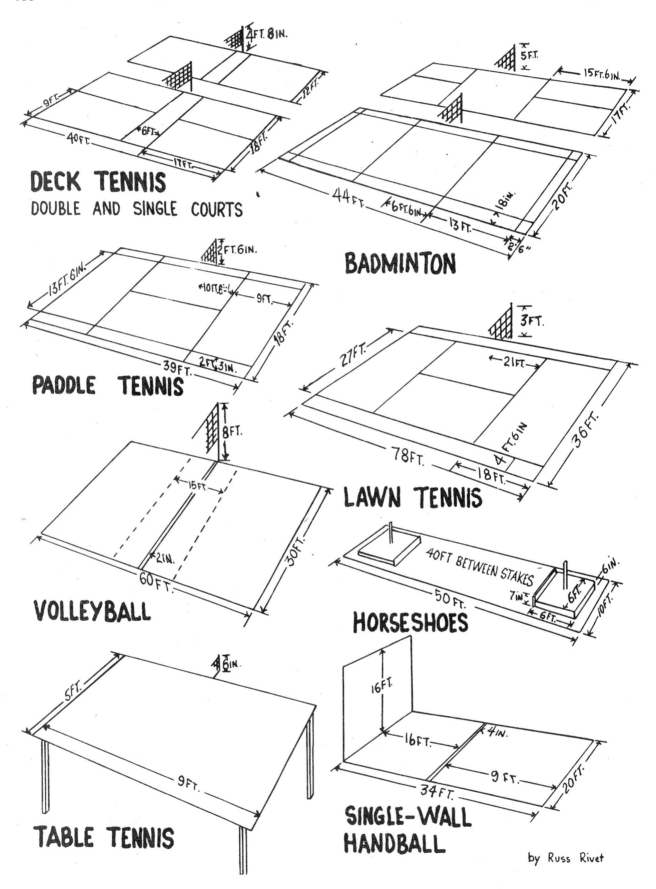

**DECK TENNIS**
DOUBLE AND SINGLE COURTS

**BADMINTON**

**PADDLE TENNIS**

**LAWN TENNIS**

**VOLLEYBALL**

**HORSESHOES**

**TABLE TENNIS**

**SINGLE-WALL HANDBALL**

by Russ Rivet

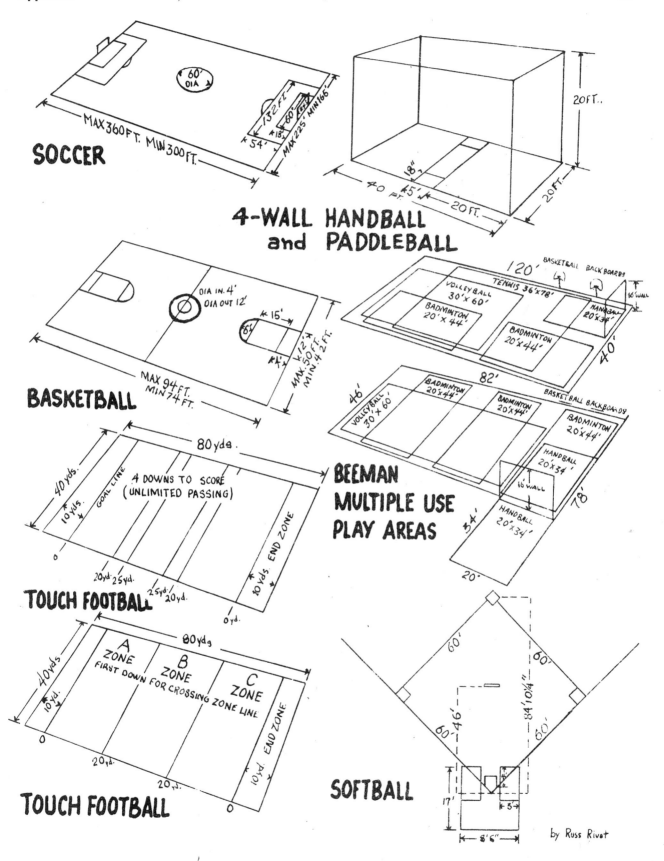

**SOCCER**

MAX 360 FT. MIN 300 FT.

**4-WALL HANDBALL and PADDLEBALL**

20 FT.
40 FT.
20 FT.
20 FT.
18"
45'

**BASKETBALL**

MAX 94 FT. MIN 74 FT.
DIA IN. 4'
DIA OUT 12'
15'
6'
4'
12'
MAX 50 FT. MIN 42 FT.

**TOUCH FOOTBALL**

80 yds.
40 yds.
10 yds.
GOAL LINE
4 DOWNS TO SCORE (UNLIMITED PASSING)
10 yds. END ZONE
20 yd. 25 yd.
25 yd. 20 yd.
0
0 yd.

**TOUCH FOOTBALL**

80 yds
40 yds
10 yd.
A ZONE
B ZONE
C ZONE
FIRST DOWN FOR CROSSING ZONE LINE
10 yd. END ZONE
20 yd.
20 yd.
0
0

**BEEMAN MULTIPLE USE PLAY AREAS**

120'
BASKETBALL BACKBOARDS
TENNIS 36'×78'
VOLLEYBALL 30'×60'
BADMINTON 20'×44'
BADMINTON 20'×44'
HANDBALL 20'×34'
16' WALL
40'

82'
46'
VOLLEYBALL 30'×60'
BADMINTON 20'×44'
BADMINTON 20'×44'
BADMINTON 20'×44'
BASKETBALL BACKBOARDS
HANDBALL 20'×34'
16' WALL
HANDBALL 20'×34'
34'
20'
78'

**SOFTBALL**

60'
60'
60'
60'
46'
84'10¼"
17'
3'
8'6"

by Russ Rivet